TACTICAL ESPIONAGE ACTION

METAL GEAR SOLID 2
SONS OF LIBERTY
OFFICIAL STRATEGY GUIDE

W9-AOP-840

TABLE OF CONTENTS

SOLID TACTICS

300010

001236 02001255

SOLID TACTICS

Any top-level operative must understand the basics of infiltration, as well as more advanced survival tactics. This briefing is designed to unify the methods and terminology of field agents at various levels.

BASIC CONTROLS

CONTROL	FUNCTION
Left Analog Stick/Digital Pad	Movement / First Person View Control
Right Analog Stick	Adjust Camera in Corner View / Blade Attacks
SELECT	Use Codec / Exit Codec
START	Pause Game / View Map of Big Shell
⊗	Crouch to Crawl or Stand from Crouch / Cancel / Exit Codec
◯	Punch / Knock on Wall / Confirm Action / Swim
▢	Use Weapon / Throw or Choke Enemy
△	Action Button (Various Uses)
R1	First Person View
L1	Run While Shooting / Defend with Blade
R2	Right Weapon Menu—Tap to Equip or Unequip Last Weapon
L2	Left Item Menu—Tap to Equip or Unequip Last Item

Controller Flexibility

At various times and during the mission, the operative's controller buttons will take on different functions, depending on the type of environment the agent must infiltrate, what items are being used, and which weapon is equipped. For details on weapon- and item-specific controls, please turn to the appropriate chapters.

DIFFICULTY LEVEL

When beginning a game of *Metal Gear Solid 2*, there are four choices of difficulty level. After the game has been "cleared," Extreme difficulty becomes available.

Very Easy

This mode is the choice for players who are unfamiliar with the action genre. The fewest number of enemies are present, patrolling guards move and turn more slowly, and the various alert modes last for much shorter periods of time. Your character can carry vast quantities of items and ammunition. During the "Plant" chapter, all maps for the Big Shell are downloaded from the first local network Node. There is no need to download the map for every level. Boss enemies take greater damage from the player's attacks, and your character receives less damage from enemies.

Easy

This mode is designed for players familiar with action games who just haven't played Konami's *Metal Gear* series games before. Compared to Very Easy mode, a few more enemies are present. Slightly fewer items and quantities of ammunition can be carried. During the "Plant" chapter, each level's map has to be downloaded from the local network Node. Boss enemies are slightly tougher.

Normal

This is the mode at which *Metal Gear Solid 2* is meant to be played. Designed for veterans of the *Metal Gear* series of games. Virtually each small area has an enemy on patrol. Boss enemies are at their regular strengths and weaknesses. New items can be unlocked by completing a game in Normal difficulty.

Hard

For players who have cleared the full game, are familiar with the layout and patrols of each area, and are looking for more of a challenge. More enemies are encountered, areas are patrolled more quickly, and patrol routes are less predictable. Enemies have a wider and longer cone of vision.

Extreme

Becomes available after any other difficulty level is cleared. Most areas have too many enemies to sneak past. Your character can carry only one of each item and one clip of ammunition for each weapon. For die-hard gamers who aren't frustrated easily.

Game Over When Discovered

On Hard and Extreme difficulty levels, there is an extra option to end the game whenever your character is discovered. Since death is nearly inevitable if detected in either of these modes, you can avoid the hassle of attempting to fight your way clear.

MOVEMENT

Like many other buttons, the character movement control is pressure-sensitive. The operative must have a steady hand and a gentle touch when necessary. By pressing the Left Analog Stick or Digital Pad in any direction, the character moves in that direction. When the Left Stick is pressed to its extent of motion, the character will run. Pressing the Left Stick just slightly in the desired direction causes the character to "sneak."

"Sneaking"

The object of *Metal Gear Solid 2* is to infiltrate deep into enemy territory, unseen and undetected. If the character runs over iron gratings, down stairs, or across other areas where his footsteps can be heard, the sound may alert guards to the intruder's presence. To pass unheard, use the "sneak" method to move over gratings and other tricky areas by pressing the Left Analog Stick very lightly. Another way to move across gratings and other hazardous floor areas quietly is by crouching and crawling across them.

Crouching

While standing still, press  and the character will crouch. This position is useful for hiding behind low crates and other waist-high obstacles, to hide from enemy patrols, or to see better around corners or behind boxes. From this position, use the movement control to enter crawling position.

Crawling

When the character is crouching, press the movement control in any direction to make the character flatten out on the ground. The character will crawl across the ground on his stomach in the direction you press. To turn the character, rotate the Left Stick in a new direction. Crawling is useful for entering vents, moving under obstructions, and for silently crossing floor areas where the character might make noise. Press ⊗ to make the charcter stand upright.

Rolling

While moving across an area, press ⊗ and the character will initiate a roll. Each character's roll move is different. Solid Snake dives across the ground and performs a somersault. Raiden leaps foot over foot in a sort of torso-axial flip. Executed precisely, a roll may be used to dive from one corner across an open space to another corner without being seen. A roll can also knock an enemy down. But, if the enemy has already spotted the intruder, there is a better chance that the soldier will kick the character to defend against this form of attack. Raiden's torso-axial flip can also be used to jump over short gaps and to leap quickly down flights of stairs.

Swimming

When the character dives into water, the control scheme shifts to swimming mode. After the character dives or walks into the water, he will surface and tread water. While the character is on the surface, press the movement control to make him stroke across the water in the direction you desire. Press ⊙, and the character will dive underwater.

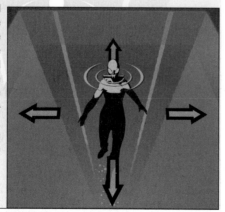

When underwater, press ⊙ to swim forward. While stroking through the water, press the movement control upward to make the character swim toward the surface. Press down to make the character swim deeper, and press left or right to make the character turn. Use the Right Analog Stick to make the character perform hard turns and flips underwater. Press left or right on the Right Stick, and the character will turn 90° left or right. Press downward on the Right Stick, and the character will flip under himself to do a 180° turn.

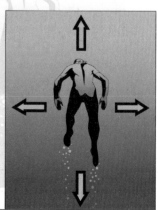

O2 Gauge

While underwater, the character's **O2 Gauge** will be displayed. The O2 Gauge is a reading of how much oxygen is left in the character's lungs. While underwater, the O2 Gauge decreases. If the character's Life Meter is not full, the O2 Gauge will decrease more rapidly. When the O2 Gauge drops to zero, the character's life will begin to decrease. At the beginning of the "Plant" chapter, Raiden is equipped with a deep-sea diving mask that elongates the O2 Gauge. When the mask is removed, the O2 Gauge will be reduced to the normal level 1 length. The O2 Gauge can be lengthened and increased in level by swimming often and exercising underwater. While swimming underwater, press the Action button (△) to make the O2 Gauge last longer. The more you press the Action button whenever you are underwater, the more likely that the O2 Gauge will be lengthened or "leveled up."

Quick Turns Underwater

Aside from using the Right Analog Stick to make quick turns underwater, you can also make quick turns by entering First Person View mode. Rotate the First Person View to the new direction of travel, and when you release the R1 button, your character will be facing that direction and ready to swim that way.

HIDING

Since *Metal Gear Solid 2* emphasizes the need to move through areas undetected, hiding from enemies is a major factor in game play. The character can hide behind any object or environmental feature that the enemy cannot see through. This includes walls, crates, and boxes. Characters can even hide from enemies by hanging under railings as guards pass on the platform overhead. Hiding well is a skill for any player to develop in order to master the game.

Pressing Against a Wall

Enemies cannot see through walls and boxes, so if you stand just around the corner from a guard, he cannot see you. However, there is a more advantageous way to hide. Move toward any wall, and the character will turn and press his back against it. While his back is pressed against a wall near a corner, the camera angles out in front of the character. From this angle, the player is capable of seeing the area and any guards around the corner from the character. A guard is not likely to spot a character hiding behind a corner or behind a crate when his back is pressed up against it.

While the character's back is pressed against a flat surface, press ✖ to crouch. This enables the character to hide behind low, waist-high objects, such as low walls and boxes.

Side-Stepping

When the character's back is pressed against a surface, he can "side-step" left or right along the surface by angling the Movement control slightly left or right. The side-step can also be achieved by pressing L2 or R2 while pressed up against a wall.

The side-step is an extremely useful action. The player can use the side-step to move the character closer to the next corner, to angle-out the camera in order to see the next area. The side-step move can also be used to cross extremely thin ledges. While pressed up against a surface, press ✖ to crouch. The character can "crouch-step" to the left or right in the same fashion as side-stepping.

Corner View & Peeking

While the character's back is pressed up against a wall near a corner, the player can see the area around the corner. To get a better view of the area beyond the corner, press `L2` or `R2` while in Corner View in order to "peek" around the corner. The character will lean out and look at the area around the corner. While in this position, move the Right Stick to adjust the camera angle. Peeking is extremely useful when the player has opted not to use the Radar. But be cautious, because if an enemy spots your character peeking, they might sound an alarm and radio for help.

Knocking on Walls

Sometimes it is possible to "bait" an enemy into leaving his regular patrol route and moving into a more desirable position by creating a noise. To create a noise by "knocking," press the character's back against a wall or a flat surface. Then press ○ to knock. When the enemy is in a range equal to twice the length of his cone of vision, he will hear the knock and will move to investigate.

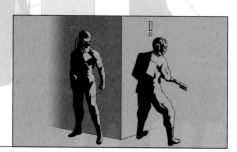

Hiding in Lockers

If the character has been spotted, and the guard is moving in to investigate, you must quickly find a place to hide your character from view. One of the best hiding spots is inside a locker. To open a locker, face it and press the Action button (△). To hide in a locker, move inside and the character will shut the door behind him. While hiding in a locker, the camera switches to "Intrusion Mode." In this forced First Person View, the character can see through the vents in the top of the locker. Press `R1`, and the character will peek through the vents more closely. But don't press the button too hard, or your character will bang his head against the door! During a "clearing," which is detailed later in this chapter, it is unwise to peek through the vents to see what soldiers are doing outside. If one of the guards happens to shine a light through the vents, he will spot you in the locker! The character can crouch inside a locker by pressing ✕. This is a safe way to hide in a locker and not get spotted through the vents.

Also, useful items are sometimes stowed in lockers. Some lockers are locked, but they can be broken into by punching the locker. If the door falls inward, then there is no item hidden in the locked compartment. But if the door falls outward, then you have most likely found a secret item! However, avoid falling locker doors.

CAMERA BASICS

Controlling the camera angle is important in *Metal Gear Solid 2*. The regular view in the game is a top-down, overhead view. Very little in front of or behind the character is visible in this angle, so it's good to learn some basic camera-using techniques. Move from corner to corner, hiding and using Corner View to scope out the next area before moving on. Unless you know for certain that you have a clear run at the next section of an area, try to stay out of the top-down view as much as possible.

Move to a wall or flat-surfaced object and press the character's back against it in order to angle-out the camera for a better view. Use this function not only to hide, but to study the layout of areas and memorize the patrol patterns and timing of guards. Also, make regular use of the First Person View mode to see an entire area from the character's perspective.

 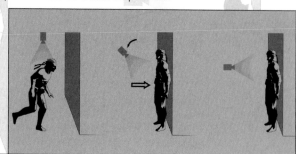

First Person View

Press and hold **R1** to enter First Person View. The camera angle shifts to the character's perspective, so that you are seeing through his eyes. First Person View is a much more flexible control option in *Metal Gear Solid 2*. While in First Person View, you can press ⊗ to crouch. Press **L2** or **R2** to strafe a step left or right. The strafe can be used to peek very quickly around corners and to dodge enemy fire. The character will stand on his tiptoes if you press both **L2** and **R2** while in First Person, allowing you to see and aim over high obstacles.

Your character can fight in First Person View if you press the Attack (⬤) button. Entering First Person prevents the character from moving, so it is usually better to stay in Third Person perspective when dealing with a boss, an attack team, or other enemies. But First Person is excellent for aiming shots at unsuspecting guards, because the point of impact on a target determines what kind of damage you'll inflict on an enemy. First Person is essential for aiming tranquilizer darts at guards, because a tranquilizer fired at the head will put a guard to sleep instantly.

Intrusion Mode

When the character crawls into a vent or hides inside a locker, the camera view automatically shifts to "Intrusion Mode." This is a sort of forced First Person View. If Radar Type 2 is in use, the Soliton Radar display will disappear when the character crawls into a vent or hides in a locker. For this reason, it is easier to use Radar Type 1 so that the Soliton display does not disappear while you are hiding in lockers and crawling through vents. You don't want to crawl out of a vent while a soldier is watching!

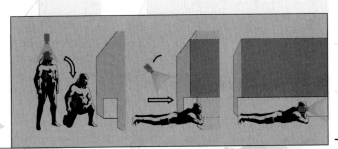

ACTION BUTTON COMMANDS

The Action button (△) has various functions, depending on what the character is facing. The Action button also gains temporary functions during certain events in the course of the mission.

Opening Doors

One of the first functions of the Action button to be explained in the game is opening watertight doors on the Tanker. When facing a watertight door, press △ and the character will start to turn the handle on the door. Tap the Action button rapidly to open the door more quickly. If enemies have spotted the character, they will shoot him each time he tries to open a watertight door.

Calling Elevators

Face the call button beside an elevator and press △ to summon it. An elevator may take some time to arrive at your level. To make the elevator come more quickly, press the Action button twice in a row.

Climbing Ladders

Face a ladder and press △. The character will climb onto the ladder. Then press the Movement control up or down to ascend or descend the ladder. If you reach a level and want to get off, stop and press the Movement control left or right to step off the ladder.

Climbing Onto Obstacles

The character can climb onto any waist-high surface by pressing the Action button. Use this to hop over obstacles in order to reach areas that you otherwise could not access.

Hanging From a Railing

As you face a railing on the edge of a platform or walkway, press △. The character will hop over the rail and hang from the edge on the other side. While the character hangs, he can shimmy along the rail left or right by pressing the Movement control. Press △ to hop back over the rail onto the platform, or press ✕ to drop from the rail to the level below.

Grip Gauge

While the character hangs from a rail, the Grip Gauge is displayed. The Grip Gauge will gradually decrease as the character hangs. If the character's Life Meter is not full, the Grip Gauge decreases more rapidly. If the character is still hanging from the rail when the Grip Gauge reaches zero, the character falls. If that happens, hopefully there is a platform not far below to break your fall.

The Grip Gauge is lengthened just slightly after each successful hang. In order to increase the level of the Grip Gauge, the character must "work out." As you hang from an edge, press L2 and R2 together to do chin-ups. After doing a certain amount of chin-ups, the Grip Gauge's level will increase—pretty cool! A leveled-up Grip Gauge can come in handy in several areas, including the Tanker's Engine Room and Cargo Holds.

Using a Node

During the "Plant" chapter, Raiden must download the map of each level from the local area network Node. He will not be able to use his Soliton Radar to survey the area or scout patrol positions until the map is downloaded. To use a Node, face it or press Raiden's back against it and press the Action button (△).

Nodes can also be used at any time to access the Options menu in order to change the game settings.

Guiding Emma

During a certain time late in the game, Raiden must lead a drugged and weary Emma Emmerich through the Shell 2 Core. In order to lead Emma, press and hold △ until she takes Raiden's hand. Then lead Emma through the enemy territory using the Movement control, keeping your finger firmly pressed on △.

While Emma accompanies Raiden, she is his "life partner." Her Life Meter appears on screen and if she dies, then the game ends. If Emma's Life Meter is low, let go of her and let her sit down for a while. Her Life Meter will gradually recuperate while she is seated.

Stubborn Emma

Sometimes Emma will refuse to cross an area. Will you spend time removing the obstacle, or should you just punch Emma until she falls unconscious and drag her?

ATTACKING

Infiltration and espionage are not the only tools at an agent's disposal. Wetworks are not recommended, but sometimes yours is a dirty job.

Using a Weapon

In order to equip any weapon located in your weapons inventory, hold **R2** and use the Left Analog Stick to scroll through the armaments you've acquired. To fire, throw, or place the weapon (depending on its intended use), press and release the Attack button (⬤). The effect of each weapon is unique.

When the Attack button is pressed, the character turns to face the nearest target. The shot is not aimed at any specific body part, but at the enemy as a whole. To aim a shot at an enemy's specific body part using a handgun, go into First Person Mode and hold ⬤. The character will auto-face the enemy and aim at his midsection. From there, adjust your aim with the Left Analog Stick or Digital Pad. When you release the button, the weapon will fire. Shots to an enemy's hands or shoulders will disable their arms and can prevent them from firing. Shots to the legs will prevent a guard from chasing you. Shots to the neck or head will kill instantly. If you are using a tranquilizer weapon, the drug will take effect more swiftly if you fire a shot at the enemy's head. If you shoot out the radio on an enemy's belt, he will not be able to radio for help or arouse suspicion.

For weapon-specific instructions and tips, refer to the Weapons chapter.

Throwing

When a character does not have a weapon equipped, he can grab and throw an enemy. If the enemy hits a wall or other object head-first, he could be knocked unconscious. To throw an enemy, run at the opponent barehanded and hit ⬤ at the proper instant. Enemies that are knocked out will be unconscious for only a short time, but you might be able to shake their Dog Tags out of them.

Choking

Without a weapon equipped, the character can grab an enemy in a headlock and choke him until he passes out. To execute this, sneak up behind a stationary enemy as close as possible without touching him. Stop just behind the vulnerable guard. Then press and hold the Attack button (⬤), and the character will grab the enemy in a chokehold.

After grabbing an enemy in a stranglehold, tap the Attack button rapidly, and your character will snap the enemy's neck.

After an enemy has been in a headlock for some time, he will pass out and slip out of your character's grip. Stars swirling around the enemy's head indicate that he is temporarily unconscious. The enemy can be disposed of, hidden, or "shaken down" for useful items and possibly even his Dog Tags.

With an enemy in a headlock, you can drag him with you some distance. If an enemy begins to struggle in your character's grip, tap ⬤ once or twice and then resume holding the button to choke him back into submission.

The Human Shield

A difficult maneuver to pull off, it is possible to grab an enemy and use him as a human shield against other enemies. When facing an attack team, if you can grab one of them and drag him away, the other soldiers will hesitate to fire.

Dragging

Once an enemy has been knocked out or tranquilized, you should drag the body out of sight and hide it in a safe location. If another enemy sees a guard's dead body, he will immediately call in an attack team and the area will be thoroughly searched. If an enemy finds a guard who has been knocked out or tranquilized, he will kick that enemy to wake him up. This is why tranquilizing an enemy is much safer than killing him.

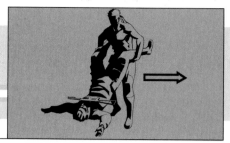

To drag an unconscious or dead enemy, stand at his head or feet and press ⬤. Without a weapon equipped, your character will pick up the guard and drag him wherever you wish using the Movement control.

Disposal Gates

Drag an unconscious or dead enemy to a disposal gate or a hole in the floor, and your character will toss the body into the waters below. Disposal gates are located on either side of the Tanker's Aft Deck, and in Strut D of the Big Shell. There are other locations where you can dispose of bodies by similar means.

"Shaking Down" Enemies

After rendering an enemy unconscious or dead, it is possible to "shake" useful items out of the enemy's body. Stand at the head or feet of a prone enemy and pick him up by pressing ⬤. Keep picking him up and dropping him until an item comes loose. If you aren't having any luck, move to the other side of the body and pick him up from there. Enemies that are unconscious are easier to shake down than enemies that are dead.

Hiding Bodies

As mentioned previously, it is very important to hide unconscious bodies. If another guard spots an unconscious soldier, he will kick him awake, and you will be forced to start over with whatever strategy you were about to attempt. This could lead to some compromising situations. However, if a guard finds a *dead* body, he will immediately call in backup support. An attack team will begin searching the area for your character. Also, if you execute a guard in a highly-traveled area, his blood will cover the floor. If another guard spots a bloodstain, he will also call in an attack team.

The best method is to tranquilize guards and quickly drag them to out of the way locations. Hide them behind low walls or obstructions where they won't be seen. If you're going to remain in an area for a while and absolutely must kill a guard, do it someplace where the mess won't be seen.

The best place to hide a guard is inside a locker. Drag a guard into an open locker, and your character will stand the body inside the compartment and close the door. Guards that are hidden in lockers will be less likely to wake up as quickly as they normally would.

Punching and Kicking

To execute punches and kicks, press ⬤. Your character will perform a combination of two punches followed by one or two kicks, depending on how many times and how rapidly you press the button. The best time to use punches and kicks against an enemy is when he has spotted you at extremely close range. If you can knock the guard out before he gets a chance to call for help, the Alert will be canceled and you'll still be safe.

Jump-Out Shot

The Jump-Out Shot is an exciting new feature in *Metal Gear Solid 2*. While standing at a corner with your back pressed against a wall or flat surface, press the Attack button (⬤), and your character will step around the corner and aim his gun at the closest enemy. If the enemy is standing with his back to the corner, the Jump-Out Shot will allow you to get the drop on the guard and possibly hold him up for his Dog Tags or other useful items.

The Jump-Out Shot works wonders in tense combat situations when your character is outnumbered. Hide around the corner from an attack team, then jump out and fire. When your character has finished the attack, he will step back behind the safety of the corner. Any time you find yourself unable to escape from an attack team, this is the tactic to use.

The Jump-Out Shot also works from a crouch position behind a wall. A variation allows you to throw grenades from the safety of the corner, without risking exposure.

Throwing Grenades from Corners

This is a great way to throw grenades without risking exposure to enemy fire. With the character's back pressed against a wall or object, equip grenades and press the L2 or R2 buttons to peek around the corner. The character will shift the grenade to the appropriate hand. Then press and hold ⬤ before releasing it. The longer you hold the button, the farther your character will throw the grenade. Don't hold it forever though, or your character might blow off his own hand!

Blade Attacks

Late in the game, Raiden acquires a High Frequency Blade. Press the Attack button (⬤) to switch between Edged style (red) and Blunt style (blue). In Edged style, hits with the Blade will kill an enemy or reduce a boss's Life Meter. Hits with the Blunt Blade will knock out an enemy or reduce a boss's purple Stun Gauge. Both styles are important. Press L1, and Raiden will defend with the sword, auto-face the enemy, and even deflect bullets just like the Cyborg Ninja!

Controlling the Blade takes a certain amount of self-control. The weapon is controlled with the Right Analog Stick. Pressing the stick up and down causes Raiden to perform uppercuts and chops. These are most effective when an enemy is attempting to defend his midsection. Don't panic and wildly press the Right Stick in every direction. Calmly think about what you are doing and press the stick, measuring each slash and the damage it does to your foe.

Pressing the Right Stick left and right commands Raiden to swing the sword back and forth. These attacks are most effective when an enemy seems to be defending or attacking from up high or down low.

Rotate the Right Stick 360°, and Raiden will perform a spin-slash. This move damages enemies in all directions, and is most effective when Raiden is surrounded.

To thrust forward with the sword, press down on the Right Stick as you would a button so that it clicks. Raiden will step out and jab the sword into his enemy. This is an excellent attack for cutting enemies from just outside their range. However, it does little damage and is more effective when combined with a series of slashes and chops.

Attack Block Extreme

The most important tip to remember about the High Frequency Blade is to keep your finger on the L1 button whenever you are not attacking. Always be ready to deflect attacks and bullets. You can also move while defending, so use this to get in close to an enemy before hacking him up!

Bleeding

When your character's Life Meter has been reduced to one fourth or less, the meter will turn reddish orange. This indicates that your character is suffering severe blood loss. The Life Meter will gradually decrease on its own until it runs dry. At that point, the next hit that your character takes will kill him. The worst part is that while he is bleeding, your character will drip blood on the floor everywhere he goes. As you try to avoid enemies, the trail of blood will lead the terrorists to your character's location. You can stop bleeding by applying a Bandage, but you will not recover health unless you use a Ration.

Another way for Raiden to stop his bleeding and recover a small amount of health is to lay flat on the floor for a time. Remaining still, the nanomachines in Raiden's blood will coagulate the blood around his wound and repair damaged tissue.

Using Rations

Rations will restore some amount of health, returning the Life Meter to its full length. To use Rations, press L2 and select them in the Left Item Menu. Press ○ while the menu is open to use a Ration.

During boss fights, it is wise to equip the Rations in the left item menu and keep them handy. With the Rations equipped, a Ration will be used automatically if your character's life is reduced to zero.

MENU BASICS

Your inventory menus are controlled with the L2 and R2 buttons. The menu on the left is the Item Menu where key cards, Rations, electronic sensors and other useful equipment is stored. Hold L2 and scroll through the items with the Movement control. When you select an item, it remains in the lower-left corner of the screen to show that it is in use. To unequip the item, tap the L2 button. Press the L2 button again to equip the last item again quickly.

The right Weapons Menu is controlled with the R2 button. This menu features items that are visibly equipped in your character's hands, so not all of them are weapons. To equip a weapon, hold the R2 button and scroll through the items with the Movement control. When the item is equipped, the icon remains displayed in the lower-right corner of the screen. To unequip a weapon, tap R2. Quickly tap the button again to equip the last weapon once more.

In the Options menu, the inventory can be made to group items by type or to display each item in its own slot, similar to the menu setup of the last *Metal Gear Solid* game.

RADAR BASICS

Beginning a game of *Metal Gear Solid 2*, the player is offered three Radar options. Two of the options determine if the Soliton Radar is displayed during Intrusion Mode or not, and there is also the option to navigate without any Radar display whatsoever. Navigating without the aid of the Soliton Radar is recommended only for expert players who have memorized the locations in the game.

Type 1 Radar

The Soliton Radar functions exactly like it did in the previous game. Your character's position and the positions of enemies are tracked in the Radar display in the upper-right corner of the screen. The radar stays on when your character is inside a locker or a vent. This is the easiest and most advantageous type of Radar to use.

Type 2 Radar

The Radar is invisible when your character is inside a locker or a vent. The display may also disappear during Caution Mode in certain areas of the game.

Electronic Jamming

The Radar will not display when electronic interference is present. Interference can be caused by equipment or high voltage electricity in the area. The detonation of a Chaff Grenade also causes Jamming. While Jamming is in effect, your character also cannot use remote control missiles, lock-on Stinger missiles, or C4 with a remote detonator. But the electronic interference also invalidates the enemy's equipment. Guards cannot radio for help, surveillance cameras cannot function, and guided missiles cannot be targeted at your character.

ALERT MODES

The *Metal Gear Solid 2* instruction manual discusses the various Alert Modes in detail. Knowing the situation of each mode is essential to survival.

An "Investigation"

In certain areas, one of the guards is required to radio in a status report every few minutes. If the guard does not radio in, an investigation is ordered. During an investigation, other guards in the area will search for the guard who is missing. If no other guards are in the area to carry out the search, then additional guards may be dispatched to the area to find out what is going on.

An investigation can be avoided by leaving an area just before the commander finishes giving the order to investigate. This will cancel out the investigation. Then you can return to the area immediately and have a few more minutes to finish your business before the next demand for a status report comes over the radio.

A "Clearing"

When a guard has spotted your character, it's time to hide. If your character hides in the same area where the guard spotted him, then an attack team is called in to search the area. The room-to-room search that takes place is called a "clearing." While a clearing is in effect, the player will notice the movement of the attack team is displayed in the window where the Soliton Radar is normally shown.

During a clearing, guards may also search in lockers and other areas that can conceal your presence if they believe that is where you are hiding. If your character is hiding in a locker, it is always safer to crouch inside just in case the guard looks through the vents.

Cancelling an Alarm

When your character is spotted, there are still ways to cancel an alarm before it occurs. When the guard is using the radio to call for assistance, use First Person View to aim at and shoot the device in is hand. If the guard gets to say a few words before the radio shorts out, an investigation team will be sent. But if you can tranquilize the guard and escape to the next area before the team is dispatched, the investigation will never take place. Then you can return to the area immediately and continue your business.

If the game enters Alert Mode, where guards have spotted your character and are attacking, you can cancel this mode by escaping through a door to another area. The alarm status will be downgraded to Evasion Mode, and the game enters Caution Mode soon thereafter. If you move from one area to the next while Caution Mode is in effect, the alarm will be ineffective in the next area.

DOG TAGS

Most of the guards that patrol areas of the game are carrying a set of Dog Tags, which can be taken from them by force. Collecting every Dog Tag in the game is a key element to unlocking secret items for use in your next game. To see if a guard is wearing Dog Tags, tranquilize or knock out the soldier and use the Thermal Goggles to view his neck area. The Camera and Digital Camera will show that you have already collected Dog Tags from a solider. More on this feature is discussed in the Items and Equipment chapter.

Capturing a Guard

The surest way to collect a guard's Dog Tags is to capture the guard by getting the drop on him from behind. If the player can determine a way to sneak up on the guard from behind and aim a handgun at the enemy, your character will yell "FREEZE!" and the guard will raise his hands in surrender. Once a guard is captured, gently release the Attack button and move directly in front of him. From this position, you can threaten an enemy and make him offer up the tags.

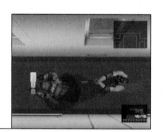

Coercing Dog Tags From an Enemy

After you have captured an enemy, and no other sentries are nearby, move directly in front of the arrested soldier and press Attack to aim the handgun at him again. Then enter First Person View and aim the weapon at the guard's head or crotch area. The guard will beg for mercy and should soon shake out his Dog Tags. Then shoot the guard and collect the tags.

Some guards will resist capture, taunting your character. These soldiers must be threatened by firing a loud warning shot at their feet or past their head. Equipping a heavy artillery weapon, such as the Stinger, the Nikita or the RGB6 will cause any guard to offer up the tags immediately, without having to aim at his body parts. If the guard does not respond to warning shots, or if the SOCOM pistol has been equipped with a suppressor, shoot one of the guard's hands or legs. Then he'll beg for mercy and offer his tags.

If you do not have strong enough firepower to threaten a guard, tranquilize him and try again later. If you stand in front of a taunting guard for too long, a twinkle appears in the soldier's eyes and he will attempt to overthrow your character!

Knocking Out a Guard

Another way to acquire Dog Tags from a guard is by knocking him unconscious. An enemy sentry can be knocked out by punching and kicking him, by throwing him, or by choking him until he passes out. A guard is shown to be knocked out when small stars circle around the guard's head. Being knocked out lasts for a much shorter time than tranquilized sleep. While the guard is unconscious, you can shake down his body for useful items. With some luck, the guard's Dog Tags will be dropped. This method is more risky than using the capture approach, and the chances of shaking out the guard's tags are slim.

Dog Tags and Difficulty Modes

Depending on which Difficulty Mode you select, there are fewer or more guards patrolling the various areas. This means that there are *fewer* Dog Tags to collect in easier modes and *more* tags to collect in harder modes! After completing the full game, use the Dog Tag Viewer to see which tags have been collected and which remain to be taken. Highlight any empty space to see which area the missing guard is patrolling. Also, you can use the Dog Tag Viewer in advance to see where new guards will be posted in Hard Mode and Extreme Mode.

Item-Specific Tips

You will find that this guide is generally crammed from cover to cover with helpful tips and fun strategies to try in *Metal Gear Solid 2*. For some interesting tips on various uses of items and weapons, some of which you may not have considered, read the Weapons chapter and the Items and Equipment chapter.

WEAPONS

Infiltrating enemy territory requires an unarmed insertion. All weapons must be acquired OSP (On-Site Procurement). Each weapon has a different use and attack method, and so the Attack button ( ) functions differently for each item. Also, some weapons have alternative uses that you might not have considered

M9 Tranquilizer Gun

An M92F customized to fire tranquilizer darts, equipped with a suppressor and laser sighting. Press ⬤ to aim, release button to fire. Releasing the Attack button slowly will cause the character to lower the weapon without firing. Shots to the head or heart knock out the subject quickly, while shots to the feet or hands knock out the subject more slowly. Can also be used to shoot out lights.

USP Pistol

A Russian 9mm handgun with laser sighting and a flashlight mounted under the barrel. Not usable with a suppressor, so noise is a factor. Press ⬤ to aim, release button to fire. Releasing the Attack button slowly will cause the character to lower the weapon without firing. In dark sections, the flashlight will come on when the weapon is aimed. The light may alert nearby patrols. In combat situations, the light may temporarily blind enemy soldiers at close range. Can be used to destroy electronic equipment, such as surveillance cameras and C4 control boxes.

SOCOM Pistol

A lightweight handgun perfect for infiltration ops, with laser sighting. A suppressor can be attached to muffle gunshot noise. Press ⬤ to aim weapon, release button to fire. Releasing the Attack button slowly will cause the character to lower the weapon without firing. Can be used to destroy cameras and C4 control boxes. Target enemy hands to negate firing abilities, and shoot guards in the legs to prevent them from pursuing you.

M4 Semi-Automatic

A heavy machinegun for use during intense combat sections against large squadrons. Uses laser sighting. Press ⬤ lightly to aim, press firmly to fire. Gun continues to fire as long as button is pressed, until clip magazine empties. Short bursts will destroy Cyphers and Gun Cameras. Continuous fire will destroy attack team riot shields. Character adjusts aim up or down to shoot high or low targets. You can also center target in First Person View, and the character will shoot the object.

AKS-74u Assault Rifle

A lightweight and versatile assault version of the standard AK-74, the favorite weapon of small armies around the world. Uses laser sighting, and can be equipped with a suppressor to muffle gunshot sounds. Press ⬤ lightly to aim, press firmly to fire. Gun fires in 10-round bursts. Will destroy most objects and defenses, same as the M4. Required in order to pose as a terrorist with the Body Disguise Uniform (B.D.U.).

PSG-1 Sniper Rifle

A compact, long-range sniper weapon with zooming scope sighting and a standard crosshair aim. When equipped, character enters First Person View, looking through the scope. Press ⬤ to zoom in, ✖ to zoom out. Aim can be steadied by ingesting Pentazemin and/or laying down on the ground. Press ⬤ to fire. The noise cannot be muzzled, so attack from long range. Zooming in closer to your target helps insure a direct hit. Target specific body parts to disable their function, or target the head for a one-shot kill. Can also be used to eliminate C4 control boxes, surveillance equipment, Gun Cameras, and Cyphers. Use in conjunction with Thermal Goggles to spot Claymores, enemy soldiers, and other targets in dark areas.

PSG-1T Tranquilizer Rifle

A customized version of the PSG-1 modified to fire tranquilizer darts instead of standard rifle rounds. Equipped with a silencer to muzzle gunshot noise. Target the head or heart to put the subject to sleep more quickly. Can also be used to destroy lights. When equipped, character enters First Person View, looking through the scope. Press ⊙ to zoom in, ⊗ to zoom out. Aim can be steadied by ingesting Pentazemin. Press ⬤ to fire.

Chaff Grenades

A silent, non-fragmenting, timed explosive that spreads a cloud of tiny metallic pieces, disrupting any electronic equipment in the area. Surveillance cameras, Gun Cameras, Cyphers, Gun Cyphers, enemy soldier radios, and mobile target lock-on tracking can be jammed by the use of a Chaff Grenade. However, the effect also negates usage of the Soliton Radar. Equip and press ⬤ to throw. Hold the Attack button before releasing in order to increase the distance thrown. Can be thrown by peeking out from behind a corner.

Stun Grenades

Also known as a "flash-bang" grenade, this non-fragmenting, timed explosive creates a sudden bright light that temporarily knocks out all enemies in range of the flash. Use in order to cross areas unnoticed or escape persecution by attack teams. However, when sentries awake, they will radio for help. Equip and press ⬤ to throw. Hold the Attack button before releasing to increase the distance thrown. Can be thrown from behind a corner by peeking out.

Grenades

Standard palm-held, timed fragmentation explosive. Instantly kills targets standing over the grenade, damages all enemies in range of the blast. Equip and press ⬤ to throw. Hold the Attack button before releasing in order to increase the distance thrown. Must be thrown in five seconds or less, or it will explode in the thrower's hand! Can be thrown by peeking out from behind a corner. Best used during heavy confrontations with small squads of enemy soldiers.

Empty Clip Magazine

An empty clip retained in the inventory. Can be thrown in order to create a small noise to distract an enemy.
Use this to make soldiers leave their patrol routes. Equip and press ⬤ to throw. Hold the Attack button before releasing in order to increase the distance thrown. Can be thrown by peeking out from behind a corner.

Book

A magazine filled with naughty pictures and articles just for men. Equip in the hand and press ⬤ to open the book and set it on the ground. Any soldier who spots the Book open on the ground will get on his hands and knees to examine it for a while. When the guard's cone of vision disappears from the radar, you may sneak around the guard quietly. Use this to bait guards into compromising positions outside their normal patrol routes, so that your character can take them by surprise.

C4 Semtex Explosive Charge (Remote Detonator)

A small block of C4 Semtex explosive wired with a remote detonator. Press the ⬤ button, and the character will set the charge at his feet. Press the character's back against a surface to set the device on a wall or a crate. Move some feet away and press ⊙ to detonate. Can be used to set up elaborate traps for guards.

Claymore Directional Sensor Landmine

A landmine with a directional sensor that explodes when an upright target enters its forward field of vision. Equip, face direction of predicted enemy approach, and press ● to set the Claymore on the ground. Use the Mine Detector or the Thermal Goggles to detect the presence of Claymores in an area. Obtain or circumnavigate Claymores by crawling across them.

RGB6 Grenade Launcher

A heavy six-shot revolving barrel grenade launcher. Lobs a grenade in a long arc. Hold ● to aim the weapon, release the button to fire. Use First Person View and raise the weapon to compensate for the arcing trajectory of the projectile. The grenade's detonation damages all enemies in range, kills enemies that are struck

Nikita Remote Control Rocket Launcher

A long-range launcher that fires a remote control fuel-propelled rocket. Press ● to aim, and press R1 simultaneously to aim in First Person View. Release Attack button to fire. When launched, the view shifts automatically to first person targeting. Guide the missile with the Movement control, turning it left or right. Changing the rocket's direction causes it to slow down. The rocket has a limited amount of fuel to propel it, and will detonate when the fuel runs out. Use the Nikita to seek out and destroy electronic and living targets in connecting corridors. Guide rockets through vents to destroy objectives.

Stinger Surface-to-Air Missile Launcher

A surface-to-air, electronically targeted guided missile launcher. When equipped, character automatically enters First Person View and looks through the tracking scope. Press R1 , and the character will hold the Stinger away from his eye, increasing peripheral vision. The Stinger uses a computerized tracking system, calculates viable target points, and marks them in the scope with small squares. The Stinger locks on to a target when the center "M" crosshair meets with a calculated targeting square. The target will turn red when a lock is acquired, and the system emits a high-pitched beeping. Press ● to fire the missile. The Stinger will lock on to aircraft, electronic surveillance equipment, and live targets, as well.

Directional Microphone

A handheld, long range sound amplification system. Can be used to penetrate walls and soundproof barriers in order to listen in on conversations from far away. Must be used to listen for a certain heartbeat during the hostage search event. When equipped, the character automatically inserts the earphone and enters First Person View. Use the Movement control to target sound source. When subtitles are turned on, the caption lettering size will increase or decrease in relation to the volume and distance of the sound. Can be used to listen to secret conversations in impenetrable rooms.

Coolant

A can of nitrogen coolant, used to freeze and defuse active bombs. When equipped, the character automatically enters First Person View. Use the Movement control to target, then press and hold ● to emit a continuous blast of cold vapor. The Coolant never runs out, but the blast will eventually lose power. The character will then shake up the can to reactivate it. When a bomb is defused, it will become covered with frost and its detonator will chime as it powers off. The Coolant can also be used to extinguish fires, drive away bugs, and to wake up unconscious enemy personnel.

ITEMS AND EQUIPMENT

In the field, specialized equipment is required to carry out surveillance operations and to sustain the operative during intense combat situations. Equip items by pressing the [R2] button and scrolling through the inventory with the Movement control. Tap [R2] to equip and unequip the last item used.

Rations

Consumable field food source that's high in protein and nutritional elements. Restores health. Press [L2] and select Rations, press ⬤ with the inventory open to use. By leaving the Rations equipped, your character will use them automatically when his Life Meter is reduced to zero.

Bandage

A gauze compress lubricated with triple antibiotic ointment. Used to stop bleeding. When a character's Life Meter is red and decreasing, use a Bandage to turn the meter green again. Press [L2] and select the Bandages, press ⬤ with the inventory open to use. No health is restored, but the operative will stop leaving a trail of blood everywhere he goes.

Pentazemin

An anti-depressant used to quell nervous tension and boost the immune system. Pentazemin can be used to steady your character's aim, to prevent sea sickness in outside areas during the "Tanker" episode, and to cure common colds by expunging harmful germs. Use in conjunction with the sniper rifles to become an expert marksman. Press [L2] and select Pentazemin, then press ⬤ with the inventory open to use.

Medicine

A highly concentrated flu remedy and nasal decongestant that suppresses cold symptoms instantaneously. However, further exposure to cold and wetness will negate the effects of Medicine. Press [L2] and select Medicine, press ⬤ with the inventory open to use.

PAN Security Card

A security card that allows the bearer to enter doors equipped with the PAN security system. Developed by engineer Hal Emmerich, the Personal Area Network system uses a person's body salts to transmit an electronic signal to a sensor built into the door. When the person bearing the card approaches, the door opens automatically. The doors are assigned levels so that access by personnel can be limited in terms of rank. Assuming you've acquired a PAN security card of sufficient level, you need only approach a secured door to open it.

MO Disk

An optical data disk containing a computer virus targeted at destroying "GW," the Artificial Intelligence of the new Arsenal Gear. The virus is modeled after the FOXDIE program, which was created by Dr. Naomi Hunter and targeted at various members of FOXHOUND, including Solid Snake.

B.D.U.

A Body Disguise Uniform that is identical to the unique uniforms worn by terrorist sentries in the Shell 1 Core. Equip in the right Item Menu to disguise your character as a terrorist while in the Shell 1 Core. Will not work in other areas of the Big Shell, because the uniform will not blend in with other guards. Must be used in conjunction with an AKS-74u in order to complete the disguise.

Body Armor

A lightweight Kevlar armor capable of deflecting a certain amount of shrapnel, cutting damage by half. When equipped in the right Item Menu, the tactical vest will appear on your character. However, the armor will deteriorate with use and becomes ineffective after sustaining constant damage. Use only in desperate situations when Rations have run out.

Cardboard Box

A cardboard box that your character can hide inside. Equip a box in the right Item Menu, and your character covers himself. Press the Movement control, and your character will move with the box on. Hold R1 and your character peeks through the handle hole in First Person View. There are six cardboard boxes in the game. Boxes must be used cleverly in conjunction with the area so as to blend in. If your character equips a box with a design that does not match the surrounding boxes or the purpose of the area, then guards will become suspicious and investigate. Cardboard Box 5, also known as the *Zone of the Enders* box, has such an attractive design that it may actually draw unwanted attention. Usage of Cardboard Boxes for hiding requires some forethought and strategy.

Scope

A long-range, lightweight set of zoom binoculars that can be used to scout great distances away. Equipping the Scope in the right Item Menu causes your character to enter First Person View as he looks through the electronic lens. Press ⬤ to zoom in and ✕ to zoom out.

Camera

A long-range zoom lens surveillance device that can be used to scout areas far away and capture photographic evidence of enemy activities. The Camera can retain up to six photographs. The memory stick is wiped clean if the shots are uploaded to the local network Node or if the game is turned off. Press ⬤ to zoom in and ✕ to zoom out. Press ⬤ to capture an image. Improving the composition of mission-critical shots will prompt exclamations of approval from your character. The Camera can also be used to determine which guards' Dog Tags have been collected. Look at the guard from a distance with the Camera and press the Action button (▲). If the guard's name appears in blue above his head, it means you have already collected his Dog Tags.

Digital Camera

A portable digital camera with a long-range zoom lens that can capture photographs and record them to your memory card. Can also be used like a Scope to scout distant areas. Press ⬤ to zoom in and ✕ to zoom out. Press ⬤ to capture a digital image. The photo save screen then appears, which allows you to save new photos or overwrite old ones. You can view your photos with the Photo Album feature, and each photo is rendered as an icon on the memory card menu. The Photo Viewer allows you to view photos, to adjust their color tones and to rename them. Press R1 to view a photo in full screen mode. The Digital Camera can also be used to determine which guards' Dog Tags have been collected. Use it to look at the guard from a distance and press the Action button (▲). If the guard's name appears in blue above his head, it means you have already collected his Dog Tags. You can find the Digital Camera late in the game, but after you complete the game in Normal or greater difficulty, it will be in your inventory at the beginning of a replay game.

Thermal Goggles

A set of electronic thermal imaging goggles that can be strapped to your character's head. When equipped, the surroundings appear filtered through an infrared field. Electronic and living materials are displayed brightly as solid images. Thermal Goggles allow you to see in the dark, and to better see electronic devices that might otherwise hide in plain sight. Thermal Goggles can also be used in First Person View.

Night Vision Goggles

A headset with light-magnifying sensors to intensify the natural lighting of any area, allowing the individual to see clearly in utter darkness. When equipped, the entire area glows green. Guards and objects that lie in the dark are rendered with enormous clarity. Unfortunately, they are almost useless underwater. Night Vision Goggles can also be used in First Person View.

003200200069

Anti-Personnel Sensor

A vibrating and sonic emission sensor that is tuned to filter out the sound of the user's heartbeat and focus on the cardiac rhythms of other nearby personnel. As enemy personnel approach, the AP Sensor will cause the controller to vibrate in warning. The vibration becomes stronger and faster as the subject approaches. For controllers without vibration technology, the device will emit a sonar beep that increases in frequency as an enemy approaches. Works automatically when your character is sealed inside a locker or crawling in a ventilation duct, but must be equipped in the right Item Menu to work otherwise. Cancels all other vibration functions when in use.

Sensor A

A bomb detection system designed and built by explosives expert Peter Stillman. The sensor detects the odors emitted by Semtex C4 bomb packages and displays them as a greenish vapor cloud on the character's Soliton Radar display. Keep this device equipped in the right Item Menu in order to narrow down the locations of C4 bombs set in the struts of the Big Shell.

Sensor B

A bomb detection system designed and built by explosives expert Peter Stillman. The sensor detects the electronic detonator signal of odorless Semtex C4 devices and beeps to indicate your character's proximity to the bomb. Equip this device in the right Item Menu when you're searching for special odorless bombs. When the frequency of the beeps increases, your character is moving closer to the explosive's location.

Mine Detector

An electronic radar enhancement system that detects the location of Claymore mines and indicates their position and direction of scanning on your character's Soliton Radar display. Keep the device equipped while moving through mined areas, and steer your character's movement around the cones of "vision" displayed on the screen. Use this device to locate and obtain Claymores.

SOCOM Suppressor

A silencer especially fitted for a SOCOM handgun. This item suppresses muzzle flash and quells gunshot noise. To attach, equip the SOCOM Suppressor in the right Item Menu and the SOCOM Pistol in the left Weapon Menu. The device will be permanently attached to the weapon. Allows the user to kill with stealth.

AKS-74u Suppressor

A silencer especially fitted for any AK series lightweight assault rifle. Suppresses muzzle flash and quiets gunshot noise. To attach, equip the AKS-74u Suppressor in the right Item Menu and the AKS-74u in the left Weapon Menu. The device will be permanently attached to the weapon. Allows the user to kill and destroy hovering Cypher devices with stealth.

Dog Tags

The number of Dog Tags that your character has stolen from guards is displayed beside this icon. Can be used in conjunction with the Dog Tag Viewer to determine how many Dog Tags remain to be obtained in the current Difficulty Mode.

1024013295001002148601 87
0147 87 37 05 011

MISSION ANALYSIS—TANKER

"Solid Snake *did* die... Either he survived, or there are *two* of them."

-Secretary of Defense, Richard Ames

1 part MISSION ANALYSIS

TANKER

On a dark and rainy New York City night two years ago, a rogue operative infiltrated the U.S.S. Discovery. He was on a covert mission to capture photographic evidence of a new top secret military project. The project centered on the development of a highly integrated weapons system designed to seek out and destroy other mobile assault systems; giant walking battle tanks called Metal Gear. The infiltrator was a highly trained and retired commando. That operative was Solid Snake, the same legendary hero who destroyed Metal Gears in three highly classified operations in the past. The first portion of the Mission Analysis will review the events that led to the sinking of the U.S.S. Discovery two years ago.

It would be best if you could get out of there without alerting anyone.

SOLID SNAKE   (David Hayter)

U.S.S.
DISCOVERY, AFT DECK

Mission Analysis:
Normal Difficulty

The entire Mission Analysis describes Normal difficulty mode, and the guard patrol routes, enemy placements, and item locations correspond to that mode. Generally speaking, in easier modes, there are fewer enemies and more items to find. In harder difficulty settings, there are more enemies and fewer items to find. This means there are less or more Dog Tags to collect, respectively, as well.

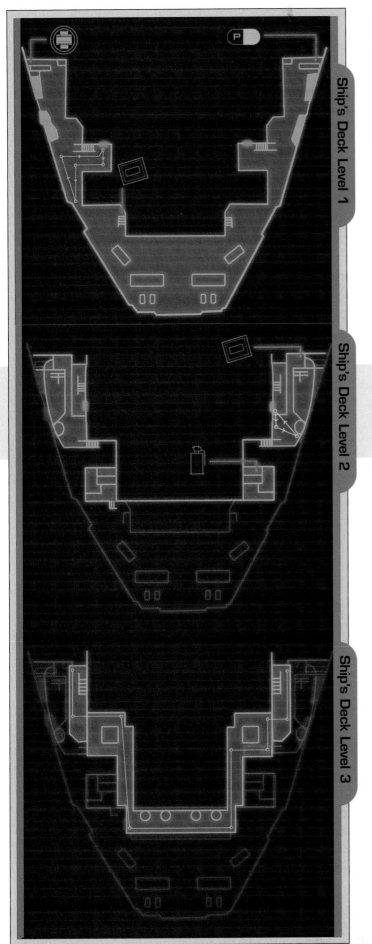

Ship's Deck Level 1

Ship's Deck Level 2

Ship's Deck Level 3

⊟	Ration
𝖯	Pentazemin
▱	Bandage
🪣	Stun Grenade

Patrol Paths

The maps in this guide are marked with guard and Cypher patrol patterns. Yellow lines represent these routes. Red dots indicate stopping points along the path. Arrows show the direction the guard travels, except in the many cases where the guard backtracks the same route in both directions

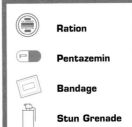

Rogue operative Solid Snake infiltrates the tanker when it crosses under the George Washington Bridge.

Snake is in contact by Codec with his long-time partner and friend from the infamous Shadow Moses Island incident, Hal Emmerich, a.k.a. Otacon. Otacon will explain several combat and control maneuvers that Snake can perform. Most of these are reviewed in the Solid Tactics chapter of this guide, and you should take all the time you need on the Aft Deck to get used to moving and controlling Snake.

This is Snake.
Do you read me, Otacon?

Members of a Russian fringe military group soon take over the tanker, eliminating the marines that were dressed like tanker workers. Snake's mission has just become a whole lot more complicated, but he is fully capable of handling it.

Ship Directions

While Snake is aboard the tanker, directions will be given in ship terminology. Therefore, as one faces the vessel from the back, the "port" side is to the left, and the "starboard" side is to the right.

Otacon, how many men do you need to take over a tanker of this size?

I'm transmitting a photo.
Let's get an ID on him ASAP.

TANKER

SOLID SNAKE

SOLID SNAKE

Known as the man who makes the impossible possible, the legendary hero who lives by the codename "Solid Snake" is an enigmatic figure, living half in shadow and half buried in his own mythology. As a rookie, Snake was a FOXHOUND operative chosen to infiltrate the fortress Outer Heaven and destroy a new super weapon called Metal Gear. Little did he know that the person who sent him into this espionage nightmare was none other than his own superior, the man with the codename "Big Boss." After successfully destroying Metal Gear, Snake retired from FOXHOUND and spent some time as a CIA agent and mercenary for hire. Then his former commander, Roy Campbell, recalled him for another operation in the Middle East. Snake's mission involved deposing the rising dictator of Zanzibar Land, who turned out to be none other than Big Boss himself. Before defeating Big Boss for good, Snake learned that the super soldier was his genetic "father." Snake returned to his Canadian wilderness retreat and tried to drown his shameful past in bottle after bottle. But when members of unit FOXHOUND took over the nuclear disposal facility on Shadow Moses Island, Campbell came calling for Snake again. This time, Snake found himself pitted against otherworldly super beings enhanced by genetic tampering. The leader of FOXHOUND was revealed to be "Liquid Snake," Solid Snake's own genetic brother and the spoiled outcast of the "Les Enfants Terrible" super soldier project. After destroying the new Metal Gear REX and eliminating Liquid during an intense car chase, Snake went into deep hiding with his new partner, Metal Gear REX engineer Hal Emmerich. The two men have worked hard over the past few years to create the first anti-Metal Gear political group, called "Philanthropy." Now Snake and Otacon need photographic proof that the Marine Corps is developing a new amphibious Metal Gear. Snake and Otacon proceed to New York City, where the ship carrying such proof is scheduled to travel through the Hudson.

3 2 0 0 2 0 0

■ 6 0 7 2 0 1 2 0 8 6 8

HAL EMMERICH,
a.k.a. "OTACON"

During the events on Shadow Moses Island, Solid Snake saved Hal Emmerich from the mysterious Cyborg Ninja. The two men could not be less alike. While Snake had the cold and detached attitude of a heartless mercenary, Emmerich was an upbeat and optimistic scientist. Another difference was Hal's somewhat childish love of Japanese Anime. Emmerich adopted the nickname "Otacon," taken from the Otaku Anime Convention, which occurs in Japan every year. Snake now refers to him solely by this name. Snake revealed to Otacon that he had been deceived by Armstech president Kenneth Baker into creating a prototype weapon of nightmarish proportions, the nuclear-equipped walking battle tank named Metal Gear REX. Emmerich's family has a dark history in science; his ancestors were responsible for the atomic bomb, among other twentieth century weapons of mass destruction. The news wounded Otacon deeply, and he resolved to help Snake destroy REX. After a tense battle with FOXHOUND leader Liquid Snake, they escaped Shadow Moses together. Since then, Otacon has worked with Snake to create the anti-Metal Gear coalition called "Philanthropy." Recently, Otacon was able to convince the United Nations to recognize "Philanthropy" as a legitimate political organization. But further proof of covert Metal Gear development is required to make the dream of "Philanthropy" into a reality. Snake and Otacon infiltrate the military installations and facilities of the world, delving into their compounds through stealth and cyber hacking. In a sense, Snake is the brawn and Otacon is the brains behind "Philanthropy."

O

OH₄

H

OTACON

1 0 2 4 0 1 3 2 9 5 0 0 1 0 0 2 1 4 8 6 0 1 8 7
0 1 4 7 8 7 3 7 0 5 0 1 1

"Philanthropy"

During the Shadow Moses Island operation, FOXHOUND spy Revolver Ocelot, a.k.a. "Shalashaska," stole an optical data disc that Solid Snake obtained from Armstech president Kenneth Baker shortly before his untimely death. The disc contained the combat test data from the Armstech prototype weapon Metal Gear REX. Ocelot sold this information on the black market, and now every superpower and third-world military is starting a Metal Gear program. During the cover-up operation to obscure the highly controversial Shadow Moses incident two years ago, Snake and Otacon split off and formed their own anti-Metal Gear organization to expose the truth about the covert Metal Gear operations around the world. Their organization obtained backing from private sources, most of whom remain anonymous. Naming their organization "Philanthropy," Snake and Otacon are now officially recognized by the United Nations as a legitimate anti-Metal Gear coalition. But their political status and influence are still lacking, and they are considered "fringe." Obtaining photographic proof of a new Metal Gear being developed by the Marine Corps will help establish the legitimacy of "Philanthropy."

Codec Chatter

141.12

OTACON

Saving Your Game

140.96

OTACON SAVE

Use frequency 140.96 to let Otacon know that you want to save your game data. Sorry, you won't be able to flirt with Mei Ling this time around.

Otacon acts as Snake's intelligence advisor on this mission. Call him to get several useful strategies for getting inside the ship, as well as surviving the entire game. If you want to know more about your equipment and weapons, use the R2 and L2 buttons to equip Snake, and then call Otacon.

Starboard
Reconnaissance

Move to the starboard side and ascend the first set of steps. Press △ to get over the rectangular obstacle here, and collect the box of **Chaff Grenades**. From this position, Snake can get the drop on the guard patrolling the second level of the starboard deck. Search the covered portion of the starboard lower deck, behind the disposal gate, to find a box of **Pentazemin Benzodiazepine Anti-Depressant** hidden in the small space behind a winch drum.

There is a door that leads to Deck-B on the second starboard level. Entering the ship through this door can greatly cut down on your game time, but you'll miss some items on Deck-A. This Mission Analysis will explore Deck-A before Deck-B, so wait to enter the door on the lower port side deck. Further back on starboard level 2, there is another small alcove where you can obtain a **Bandage**.

Otacon Informs

141.12

OTACON

For detailed information on the weapons and items you are carrying, equip them in Snake's slot with the L2 or R2 buttons and call Otacon on the Codec. He will tell you specifics on each item, as well as various uses for them that you might not think of on your own.

Port Side Reconnaissance

Approaching from the rear portion of the Aft Deck, search under the first set of stairs for a **Bandage**. Ascend the stairs and use First Person View (R1) to spot the lone guard patrolling the lower deck. The door at the bottom of the stairs leads to Deck-A, and it is the preferred way of entering the ship. Continue back along the lower deck, past the disposal gate, to a small alcove at the rear, where Snake can obtain a **Ration**.

Flu Alert!

It's possible for Snake to catch a cold if he remains on the rainy Aft Deck for too long. If Snake sneezes in the presence of enemies, he might be discovered. Alleviate his symptoms by taking a Pentazemin. In addition to steadying nerves when aiming a sniper rifle, Pentazemin also adds a boost to the bloodstream. However, the effects may only be temporary depending on how long it takes you to administer the medicine after the first sneeze.

P

Aft Deck Tactics

Each section of the Tanker Mission Analysis will have a separate section wherein we will discuss the strategies and tactics for eliminating enemy sentries. Such tactics sections will be distinct from the "Reconnaissance" portions.

Cleaning Crew

When you knock out a guard, it is imperative to dispose of or hide his body. Otherwise, he might wake up and discover Snake, or other guards might be sent to investigate his lack of reports. Drag him to one of the gates on either side of the ship. Snake will open the gate and toss the enemy overboard. Don't forget to "shake down" the guards first for useful items!

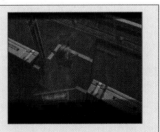

Dog Tag Strategies

Tranquilizing guards and ducking into the shadows isn't the only way to move through areas. By studying each situation, Snake is capable of surprising and capturing enemies if he can draw his gun on them at close range, from the side or from behind them. For more information about Dog Tags and how to surprise guards from behind, please consult the Solid Tactics chapter of this guide.

Top Aft Deck Guard

From Snake's starting position on the rear portion of the Aft Deck, you should be able to look up to the top deck in First Person View (R1) and see a guard patrolling the edge...

Top Aft Deck Guard, Tactic 1

Use First Person View (R1) to look at the top deck, and shoot the guard with a tranquilizer. You may have some difficulty seeing past the glare of the sentry's flashlight beam. However, you should just barely be able to make out the silhouette of the guard's head when you're aiming.

Dog Tag Difficulty

You'll note that we've accompanied each "Dog Tag strategy" with a difficulty rating. This is our way of describing, in relative terms, how easy or hard it is to obtain each set of Dog Tags. These ratings should not be confused with the game's difficulty settings.

Top Aft Deck Guard, Tactic 2

There is a way to bring the top guard down to the Aft Deck, so that he is easier to dispose of through one of the gates on either side of the deck. Use First Person View (R1) to spot the guard on the top deck, then shoot out the light on the wall directly below him. If shooting the lights doesn't attract him, then press up against the wall directly beneath his position and knock (◯). If this doesn't get his attention, then just run around on the Aft Deck like until the sentry spots Snake. Watch to see which side the guard is descending, and hide behind one of the anchor winches on the opposite side by crouching (✕). As the guard searches the deck, step out and tranquilize him in the neck.

DOG TAGS: Top Aft Deck Guard
Difficulty: Easy

There are many ways to get behind this guard. Most of them require that you move all the way up to the top deck. There are deep alcoves that Snake can hide in, so just press your back against a wall in a niche as the guard passes. Once Snake has a clear run at taking the guard from behind, step out and aim your weapon. Try to catch the guard when he is crossing an open stretch, rather than standing against the rail. Capturing him is useless if there is no room for Snake to get in front of him.

Starboard Guard

A guard searches the bay with binoculars from starboard Aft Deck Level 2. If you want to collect the items in the area or enter the ship at Deck-B, this guard must be eliminated...

Starboard Guard, Tactic 1

Ascend the first set of steps on the starboard side. Press ▲ to hop onto the rectangular obstacle, and then aim the M9 at the guard's skull to tranquilize him instantly. If the guard moves out of sight momentarily, wait until he comes back and raises his binoculars again.

Starboard Guard, Tactic 2

This method takes a bit longer, but makes it easier to dispose of the body. Shoot the wall behind the guard, causing him to turn and investigate. Shoot again further down the wall, causing him to descend the steps. When he's at the bottom, tranquilize him. Then drag him to the starboard gate for disposal.

DOG TAGS: Starboard Guard

Difficulty: Very Easy

This is one of the easiest Dog Tags to collect in the game. The soldier stands at the rail for a long time looking through his binoculars and then goes to examine a door. While the sentry looks through the binoculars, move quietly up the stairs behind him by gently pressing the Left Stick. When the guard turns to head for the door, run up behind him and press ● to get the drop on him easily! Start collecting Dog Tags with this guard to get an idea of how it's done.

Port Side Guard

One guard patrols near the lower entrance into the ship at the bottom of the port side stairs. To enter Deck-A, this guard must be compromised...

Port Side Guard Tactic

Ascend the first set of steps on the port side, hop onto rectangular obstacle, and *crouch* (⊗). If you don't stay low, the guard might spot you. Wait until the guard is standing in front of the door, and then tranquilize him. "Shake down" the guard for useful items, then drag him to the port side disposal gate.

DOG TAGS: Port Side Guard

Difficulty: Easy

Ascend to the small platform on the port side by using the first stairs. Hop over the rectangular object and stand near the rail. Watch the guard carefully. When he leaves the bottom of the stairs and heads to the left, leap over the rail, drop, and run up behind him. While this tactic seems extreme, the guard pauses for so long at each corner of his route that he becomes an easy target.

900175034   08415
0139801010021700397

11370   02006

U.S.S. DISCOVERY, DECK-A

Deck-A Crew's Quarters Reconnaissance

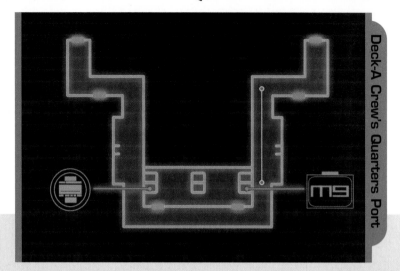

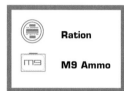

	Ration
M9	M9 Ammo

Deck-A Crew's Quarters Port

Several hidden program events are located on Deck-A. In the videogame industry, the standard term for these is "Easter Eggs." You can find the first Easter Egg by moving left from the watertight entrance to Deck-A. Try to open the sealed door at the end of the corridor, and Snake will accidentally pull off the handle!

Move to the right from the entrance and down the corridor until you reach the first automatic sliding door. Inside the crew locker room, you can search lockers when you stand in front of them and press △. The first locker on the far-left wall contains a **Ration**. There's a rather alluring pinup poster inside the door of the second locker on the far left. There are several weird things you can do with this if you're perverted enough...

The only other item is in the first locker on the far-left side of the room, a box of **M9 Bullets**, which usually adds 15 shots to your inventory. Use First Person View and you'll notice another pinup girl plastered on the inside of the door.

KONAMI EYES GIRLS

The poster girl in the black swimsuit is from KONAMI EYES, a Konami publication in Japan. There are some funny things to do with this poster. First, get inside the locker and close the door. Use the Left Analog Stick to look down at the girl and press R1 *. Snake makes a smooching sound and kisses the poster! Now leave the locker door open, stand directly in front of the poster and go into First Person View. While holding* R1 *, press SELECT and call Otacon. A funny Codec conversation happens. Also with the locker door open, press Snake's back up against it. With a weapon equipped, position Snake so that when he knocks on the door (⬤), he taps her chin. Tapping on the poster in this manner makes a funny sound! Also, equip the camera and take a picture so that the entire poster is captured in the shot. If Snake says "Goooood," then you know it's the right shot. Otacon will appreciate it later, as well...*

The second poster has all the Easter Eggs of the other pinup. Plus, you can cause something really funny to happen. Unequip Snake's weapon, press his back against the door, and position him so that his right hand is touching her leg. Press ⬤ to knock on the poster, and the pinup gets offended! Her reaction alerts the guard outside, and an attack squad will storm the locker room. Quickly get inside the locker and stay quiet to avoid detection. It's risky, but seeing the poster react to Snake's advances is quite amusing.

Locker Strategies

OTACON

141.12

While you're in the locker room, call Otacon several times. He provides Snake with valuable tactics regarding the lockers. Not only can Snake hide in the lockers, but he can also hide enemy bodies in them. In a firefight, Snake can use the locker door as a shield if it is far enough back from the door.

Deck-A Crew's Quarters Tactics
Deck-A Crew's Quarters Guard

A lone guard patrols the corridor leading to the forward portion of Deck-A. Unlike the guards on the Aft Deck, Snake cannot simply sneak around this one; a takedown of some sort is required.

STRATEGY

Deck-A Crew's Quarters Guard, Tactic 1

Press up against the wall near the corner and equip the M9. When the guard pauses in his route next to Snake, press ⬤. Snake will jump out and tranquilize the guard directly in the face. Of course, the guard will be alarmed, but he'll have no time to radio for help due to the speed of the serum.

STRATEGY

Deck-A Crew's Quarters Guard, Tactic 2

When the guard is at the top end of the corridor, shoot the wall behind him. The fool will turn to the side and wonder what happened, giving you ample time to perfectly aim a tranquilizer at his head.

DOG TAGS: Deck-A Crew's Quarters Guard

Difficulty: Very Easy

Press Snake's back against the lower corner outside the locker room, as in Tactic 1 above. When the guard turns and heads north, run after him until Snake is in close range. Press ⬤ to capture him, then simply run around the guard and aim your gun at his head—it's that easy!

Deck-A
Crew's Lounge
Reconnaissance

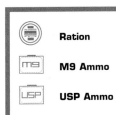

- 🔲 **Ration**
- M9 **M9 Ammo**
- USP **USP Ammo**

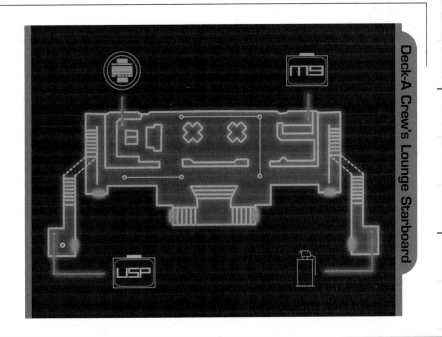

Deck-A Crew's Lounge Starboard

Entering the corridor outside the Lounge area, Snake spots two guards patrolling near the bottom of the stairs. Snake must get up to the tanker's Bridge using those stairs, so you'll have to deal with these guys!

There's a descending stairway in the starboard corridor with a box of **Stun Grenades** at the bottom. The auto-sliding door leads to the Engine Room. Although there are more items to find there, you cannot collect most of them until you have a USP. For this reason, we'll examine that area later in the Mission Analysis.

Use the methods outlined in the following Tactics section to put the guards to sleep. Then search behind the bar for **M9 Bullets**. There is a **Ration** among the couches in the Lounge area. Also, notice the scrolling image on the widescreen television on the port side wall—it's Metal Gear RAY, stowed in the tanker's hold! As you're staring at the screen in First Person View, call Otacon to have a discussion.

The corridor on the far side of the Lounge also has a descending stairway with a dozing guard at the bottom, who is swarmed by flies! There's a box of USP Bullets nearby, but you cannot obtain them until you have the USP pistol.

The Swarm!

It's best to deal with the fly-infested Russian later on, and we'll go into more detail at the appropriate time. However, if you insist on confronting him now, be swift and get away quickly. If Snake takes too long to dispatch the dozing guard, the flies will swarm around Snake. The flies can draw guards' attention, making it difficult to hide behind corners. To get rid of them, you must run away from them and quickly exit the area before the flies catch up.

Lounging Around

OTACON

While you're standing outside the lounge in the starboard stairwell, contact Otacon, and he will point out the steam pipes in the ceiling. Shooting these in a crisis situation can distract guards just long enough for you to escape.

Deck-A Crew's Lounge Tactics

Deck-A Crew's Lounge Guards (Both)

Two guards patrol in front of the staircase leading up to Deck-B. Snake must knock out these guards to continue the mission with stealth. *Do not let yourself get spotted in the Lounge*, or a large attack team will respond. Although fighting in the Lounge is actually pretty cool because there are so many glass items to obliterate, the odds of survival are slim with only the M9 for defense.

STRATEGY

Deck-A Crew's Lounge Guards Tactic

Standing in the starboard corridor outside the lounge, use First Person View to aim at the most distant guard, but wait to shoot until the closest guard follows his route back toward the bar area. When the furthest guard walks to his furthest point away and turns back, tranquilize him in the face so that he drops out of sight. Stay in First Person View, wait for the second guard to walk into view, and tranquilize him in the head as soon as he stops in front of you.

2002001519371002140501 9   01 5

DOG TAGS: Deck-A Crew's Lounge Guards (Both)

Difficulty: Medium

Collecting Dog Tags takes a serious turn for the worse. With Snake positioned just outside the lounge, as in the previous tactic, notice that when the starboard guard comes into view, the port side guard is out of his cone of vision. Quickly run up behind the starboard guard, capture him, threaten him, tranquilize him, grab the tags, and drag the body into the starboard stairwell. With him out of the way, follow the port side guard until Snake can duck into the alcove under the stairs on the left. Before the guard turns around and heads back, fire a dart at the window to create a small hole. When the guard returns, he will notice the hole and move further into the room. Step out of the alcove and capture the guard—that's two tags in one desperate strategy!

Deck-A Crew's Lounge Stairwell Guard

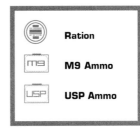

The dozing guard at the bottom of the port side stairs is not worth messing with until you have the USP later in the game. We will provide tactics at the proper time.

U.S.S. DISCOVERY, DECK-B
Deck-B Crew's Quarters Reconnaissance

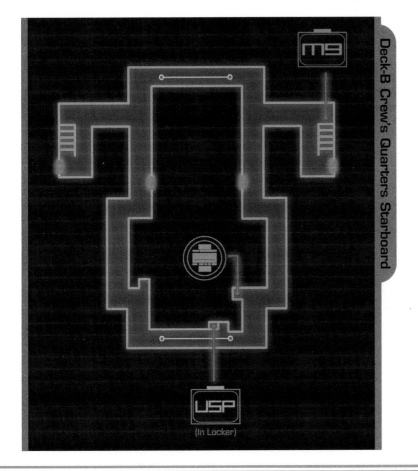

Deck-B Crew's Quarters Starboard

(Ration icon)	**Ration**
M9	**M9 Ammo**
USP	**USP Ammo**

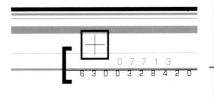

In the starboard corridor, move upward and Snake will spot the shadow of a guard around the corner.

The Shadow Knows

This is the first and the last time that a shadow is pointed out to you, so be sure to look for guards' shadows around corners from now on. On this level, you should really concentrate on getting the two guards' Dog Tags now while the time is ripe. Things won't be so advantageous later.

Move left to the starboard stairwell. The lower watertight door leads back out to the Aft Deck, so this is the other possible entry point into the ship. There's a box of **M9 Bullets** hidden in the small niche under the stairs. From here, head back down the corridor and around a few corners. There's a **Ration** in a tiny, dark alcove near the bottom corner.

In the rear portion of Deck-B, a lone guard patrols the corridor in front of a locker. There's a box of USP Bullets inside the locker, so you should hold off from attacking this guard until after you have the proper weapon.

Deck-B Crew's Quarters Tactics

Deck-B Forward Hallway Guard

Snake spots the shadow of a guard positioned at the corner. Since the enemy is temporarily stationary, it is easy to "hold up" the guard. But you have to get the drop on him before he resumes his patrol route...

DOG TAGS: Deck-B Forward Hallway Guard

Difficulty: Very Easy

This guard is really easy to "hold up," and you can acquire this guard's Dog Tags! Use the step-out attack from the corner directly behind him. After he raises his hands, gently remove your finger from the ● button so that Snake lowers the gun without firing. Move to the guard's front side and aim the gun at him again. In First Person View, point your gun at his head or crotch to make him bribe you with useful items and his tags. Then tranquilize him.

Deck-B Rear Hallway Guard

A lone guard patrols the lower portion of the corridor on Deck-B. At a later time, this guard must be silenced to obtain the much-needed USP Bullets in the locker.

6 5 0 2 1 1 7

0 2 0 2 0 0 1 5 5 6 0 1 0 1 0 0 2

DOG TAGS: Deck-B Rear Hallway Guard

Difficulty: Easy

Move to the starboard side of his patrol route. As he is walking toward port, move into the small alcove where the locker stands. When the guard stops in front of Snake's hiding spot, press and hold ●, and you will get the drop on the guard. Make your way to his front and enter First Person View. Aim at his head to make him cough up his Dog Tags and other items. Tranquilize him and stuff his body into the locker for safe keeping.

U.S.S. DISCOVERY, DECK-C
Deck-C Crew's Quarters Reconnaissance

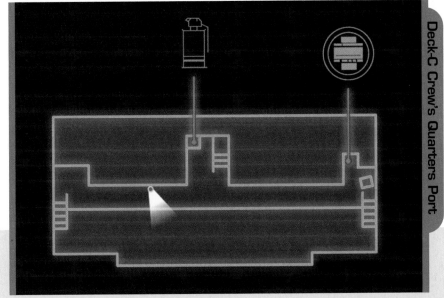

	Ration
	Chaff Grenades

Snake notices a surveillance camera mounted in the hallway. There is a locker containing **Chaff Grenades** in the center area. At the opposite end of the corridor, near the stack of crates, there is a floor-level duct where a **Ration** has been stashed. When you're finished in this corridor, ascend the stairs to Deck-D.

Camera Weaknesses

141.12

OTACON

After Snake notices the camera, immediately call Otacon on the Codec for some tips on how to deal with cameras.

Deck-C Crew's Quarters Tactics

A surveillance camera is mounted high on the wall in the corridor. Snake is not capable of destroying the device with only a tranquilizer gun, so some other means of circumnavigating the camera is required. If Snake is spotted, an attack team will flood the narrow corridor.

STRATEGY

Deck-C Camera Tactics

There are two ways to get past the device. The easiest way is to use a Chaff Grenade, which will cause electronic interference and temporarily blind the camera. Run past the camera before the effect subsides. The other way to get around the electric eye is to press Snake up against the wall under the camera and side step along the wall directly under it. All cameras have a blind spot directly under them. Since this camera doesn't pan back and forth, sliding under it unnoticed is relatively easy.

Deck-C Attack Team Tactics

If the camera spots Snake, a small attack team will be dispatched to find him. With some luck, you might reach the locker positioned beside the stairs up to Deck-D. But a better way to fight is to return to the port side stairs. If the soldiers spot you in this small area, shoot the fire extinguisher by the doorway to distract them. Then use First Person View and tranquilize the two or three responding guards.

U.S.S. DISCOVERY: DECK-D
Deck-D Crew's Quarters Reconnaissance

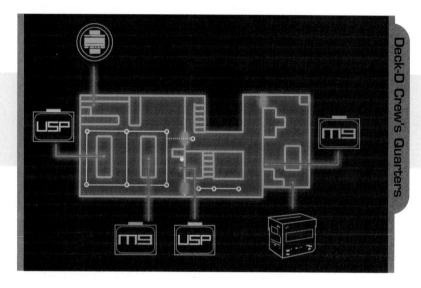

Deck-D Crew's Quarters

🖥	**Ration**
USP	**USP Ammo**
📦	**Box**
M9	**M9 Ammo**

This area is heavily patrolled and surveyed, so watch your step more carefully than ever! As Snake comes up the stairs, a guard enters the Mess Hall. Don't move until he's inside and the door closes behind him. Then proceed to the doorway, cross the threshold into the cafeteria, and tranquilize the guard from a distance. There is a **Ration** behind the kitchen counter. Crawl underneath the table closest to the door for **M9 Bullets**. There is a box of USP Bullets under the table furthest in, but you'll have to wait until Snake has the USP.

Another box of USP Bullets is under a surveillance camera, so it's better to wait until later before you attempt to get these items. The door just south of the camera leads to the stairs up to the Bridge, but the vigilant camera and the guard posted just beyond the doorway make it difficult to use this route. You are better off exiting the Mess Hall through the same door you entered.

02001255

Crossing the corridor to the starboard side, Snake receives an urgent Codec transmission from Otacon. The corridor is rigged with Semtex plastic explosives, set to go off when anything crosses the invisible infrared detection beams. Snake must find some way to get around them.

As you face the IR beam trap, the doorway leading into the food pantry is behind you. At the back of this room, Snake can collect **M9 Bullets** and **Cardboard Box 1**. When the latter item is equipped in the Item Menu (**L2**), Snake will crouch inside a box that looks like any ordinary orange crate. Use First Person View to see through the box's handle opening. As the name indicates, this is just the first of many area-specific cardboard boxes that Snake will acquire. This box allows you to hide specifically anywhere inside the ship. Used at any position outside the tanker, this box might actually draw suspicion.

When Snake picks up Cardboard Box 1 in the pantry, a sentry enters the room and decides to take up a guard post here. Snake must now figure out how to get out of this tricky situation undetected...

Deck-D Crew's Quarters Tactics

Deck-D Mess Hall Guard

As Snake enters Deck-D, a guard enters the Mess Hall. You must eliminate this sentry before he eventually returns this way.

STRATEGY

Deck-D Mess Hall Guard Tactic

The strategy for tranquilizing this guard is outlined in the first paragraph of the Reconnaissance section.

 DOG TAGS: Deck-D Mess Hall Guard

Difficulty: Medium

As this guard enters the Mess Hall from the corridor, immediately follow him. Try to catch up to him before he reaches his stationary position in the center of the room. As soon as Snake is in close range behind the guard, capture him and get those tags. Going for these tags certainly generates an adrenaline rush!

Deck-D Semtex C4 Trap

Moving starboard in the upper corridor, Otacon warns Snake about the explosives wired in the hallway. Snake must find a way to make infrared beams visible.

STRATEGY

Deck-D Semtex C4 Trap Tactic

First, wait until the guard patrolling the corridor near the exit pokes his head out from around the corridor, and tranquilize him. Then carefully aim at and shoot the fire extinguisher on the other side of the explosives. The scattering powder reveals a floor-level gap in the beams. An alternate way to reveal the beams is to use your Cigarettes; this is the "usual method" Otacon refers to in the Codec transmission. Crouch and crawl under the beams while they are still visible.

DOG TAGS: Deck-B Rear Hallway Guard

Difficulty: Medium

The regular strategy for taking down this guard is covered in the strategies for moving past the Semtex IR trap discussed above. Obtaining this guard's Dog Tags is another matter entirely. After you have tranquilized the Mess Hall Guard, position Snake at the bottom of the table closest to the south door. Watch the radar as the guard moves in the corridor beneath the Semtex trap. When the guard is moving *toward* Snake, throw a Chaff Grenade and wait for it to jam the camera. As the guard is moving *away* from Snake's position, run through the south Mess Hall door and move in behind the guard. Overtake him before he stops at the Semtex trap, or you won't be able to get in front of him to demand the tags.

Deck-D Pantry Guard

While Snake is inside the food storage pantry, a guard will return to his post in the room. From behind the food shelves, you must determine how to get around the guard and get on with the mission...

Deck-D Pantry Guard Tactic

Use First Person View to line up a shot at the back of the guard's head, aiming between the vegetables on the shelf. To help line up the shot, press L2 or R2 to strafe left or right. The buttons are pressure sensitive, so you should be able to align the shot just right.

Box of Tricks

If Snake is heard or if he sneezes, quickly use Cardboard Box 1 to disguise yourself. However, if the guard leaves to go get others, run up to the other boxes marked "The Orange." Try to line up your box with them, so that your box appears to be stacked alongside the others. This is an even more convincing cover.

"Clearings" Are Bad

If Snake is discovered in the pantry and the guard radios for help, the alert will bring in several more guards for a "clearing." This means that an all-out firefight is going to ensue as soon as the soldiers have sighted their target. All that stands between Snake and the enemy is the fruit on the shelf. The guards will gradually blast it away, so use step-out corner shooting to try to knock them unconscious. Don't bother aiming for the heads; you risk standing out in the open too long.

Boris is Frisky!

You cannot claim the Dog Tags of the guard who enters the pantry until you have the USP. The stubborn sentry just isn't scared until bullets whiz past his ears. We'll cover how to get this guard's tags in a later section. Until then, do not kill the guard; just tranquilize him.

U.S.S. DISCOVERY, DECK-E BRIDGE

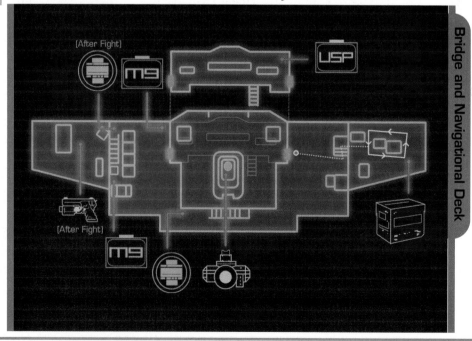

[After Fight]

[After Fight]

Bridge and Navigational Deck

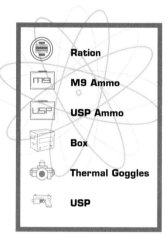

| Ration |
| M9 Ammo |
| USP Ammo |
| Box |
| Thermal Goggles |
| USP |

Finally reaching the navigational command center, Snake finds more unfortunate victims of the terrorist takeover. Moving to the computer panel, he gets the course heading that Otacon wants, indicating the motives of the intruders. Russian reinforcements arrive. The ship is now completely under their control. However, Snake abruptly cuts off communication when he notices someone standing on the port bow. Move to the watertight door and turn the wheel to open it. Be certain to have Otacon record your game data now, if you haven't up to this point!

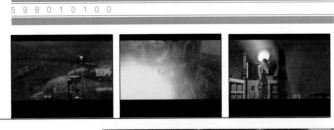

BOSS FIGHT

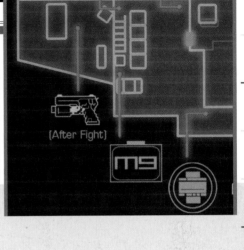

[After Fight]

Olga Gurlukovich

Gender:	Female
Affiliation:	General Gurlukovich's Splinter Faction Army
Weapon:	USP 9mm with Barrel-Mounted Flashlight

Olga's a wicked shot! Start off by moving to the crates stacked on the starboard side and press Snake's back against them so that you can see Olga hiding behind the crates nearby. Corner-shots are good enough; don't bother going into First Person View mode. You'll take more damage trying to carefully aim your shots. While Olga is trying to spot Snake, sneak over to the port side of the crates, and you should be able to nail Olga from the side where she isn't looking.

You'll find a **Ration** and **M9 Ammo** nearby in case you need them (see the map). It may seem that the M9 is no good against her, but that isn't true. Although her green life bar never decreases, each dart reduces the small purple bar. This is her "consciousness meter," and you'll win the battle if you can knock her out. After suffering a few tranquilizers, Olga moves to the back of the ship and shoots the cables holding down the tarp. Now she has great cover behind the large canvas fluttering in the wind. Olga seems able to shoot Snake straight through the tarp. To nullify her advantage, move to the open space on the far-left side, where you can use First Person View to see Olga beyond the tarp. Even better, aim for the lower-right anchor of the tarp and sever it with a shot. The wind will blow the tarp away.

If you are successful at releasing the tarp, Olga will shoot the light so that it blares in your face and makes it hard to aim at her. You must move quickly to the other side of the area, where the light is not glaring. From there, you should be able to target and shoot out the light in First Person View, but do it quickly. Olga will move the light again to blind you in your new position, and you'll have to move and start over.

When Olga seems to have Snake pinned down on one side or the other, wait until she ducks behind her cover, then move. From a new position, you should be able get at least one surprise shot to Olga's side.

Be careful when you're standing in the open spaces on the left because Olga will toss grenades to flush you out. Olga warns that she is throwing a grenade by screaming "Take this!" or something to that effect. Immediately get out of your position by rolling left or right.

Also, notice that when Olga hides at the very back of the port bow after the tarp has been removed, you can see her between the palates! In First Person View, you should be able to shoot her as many times as you want and finally knock out the savvy zhensheena.

OLGA GURLUKOVICH

Olga Gurlukovich is the daughter of one of the most formidable leaders of the former Soviet Army. Her father took her with him to Afghanistan during the Russian campaign of the late 1980s. When the situation escalated, she and her father were trapped in a remote area of the country for weeks. Colonel Gurlukovich taught his daughter how to survive, how to coerce and deceive opponents, and how to surprise the enemy even when at a disadvantage. She has retained those skills, and her subsequent military training compounds her combat abilities.

11010

015480101003120038¶

07713

630032842008²⧘   2002001519371002140501⧘   0151937100

Olga Compromised

While Olga is unconscious on the deck, stand at her feet and take a photo of her. Snake should make a "kissing" sound after the photo is taken. Retain this shot until Otacon has a chance to look at it...

Frame your shot like this for an appropriate reaction from Otacon.

U.S.S. DISCOVERY: NAVIGATIONAL DECK, WING

Olga lies unconscious on the port side deck. Now it's time to see what items the navigation crew left behind that might be useful.

Navigational Deck Reconnaissance

After the battle, Snake collects Olga's empty **USP**. "Shake" Olga's unconscious body to get her **Dog Tags**. Keep shaking her, and you might also get **M9 Bullets**. There is a **Ration** in a small pit behind the stairs.

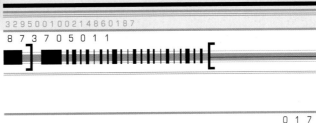

Move left to the starboard side of the Navigational Deck, and up the stairs. At the base of the ladder, press △ to make Snake climb. Press up on the Left Analog Stick, and he will climb to the top. You can find the **Thermal Goggles** there. These will be very helpful with several of the tasks ahead.

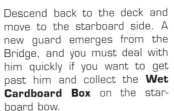

0 1 7

Descend back to the deck and move to the starboard side. A new guard emerges from the Bridge, and you must deal with him quickly if you want to get past him and collect the **Wet Cardboard Box** on the starboard bow.

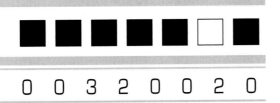

0 0 3 2 0 0 2 0

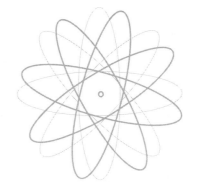

Navigational Deck Tactics
Navigational Deck Guard

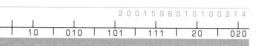

When Snake moves to investigate the starboard side of the Navigational deck, a guard gets in the way. This guard proves challenging due to the speed and relentlessness with which he patrols his route.

DOG TAGS: Navigational Deck Guard
Difficulty: Easy

After the guard emerges from the bridge, he will pause for a moment. Then he will begin patrolling the port bow very quickly, without stopping. Tranquilizing him from a distance is difficult when he moves like this. The easiest way to overtake him is during the brief instance when he pauses just outside the Bridge door. Run up behind him and hold him in place by surprising him. Since you're capturing him anyway, you might as well get the Dog Tags while you're at it!

U.S.S. DISCOVERY: DECK-E BRIDGE

Return inside, grab the **USP Bullets**, and head downstairs. Before you begin the long descent into the tanker's holds, make sure that Snake doesn't leave wet footprints everywhere, or it will give him away.

You know the layout and how to navigate the upper decks. We'll explain what changes occur on the downward trip, and how to get around the new obstacles. Until you reach the Engine Room, only the new items and tactics to use against the guards will be discussed.

U.S.S. DISCOVERY: DECK-D

With Snake entering the area from the Bridge's stairs, the guards' placement and patrol routes have changed somewhat. Remember that there are **USP Bullets** being guarded by the surveillance camera inside the Mess Hall, and more **USP Bullets** lie under the table closest to the electric eye.

Deck-D Crew's Quarters Tactics

If you didn't collect Dog Tags in this area earlier, it's going to be much more difficult now. However, now that Snake has a loaded USP, it's time to collect the tags of that mouthy Russian who likes to hang out in the pantry.

Deck-D Mess Hall Guard

The guard of the Mess Hall now stands a little closer to the south door, so he is very likely to spot Snake if you just charge carelessly into the room.

STRATEGY
Deck-D Mess Hall Guard

Watch the Soliton Radar in the upper-right corner of the screen. As soon as the guard turns his attention to the port side of the room, away from the south door, move to just outside the south door so that it opens. Then aim the gun, enter First Person View and aim the shot at the guard's head.

Deck-D Corridor Guard

Move to the south side of the IR beams and use First Person View to see the guard on the other side. Wait until he pauses within your sight, then aim a shot at his head and tranquilize him.

Deck-D Surveillance Camera

With both guards tranquilized, equip the USP and step just inside the Mess Halls' south door. Press Snake's back against the south wall, so that he stays out of the camera's range. Then enter First Person View and aim a shot at the camera. The bullet will deactivate the device, so you can freely grab the USP Bullets that sit under it.

DOG TAGS: Deck-D Pantry Guard

Difficulty: Hard

The only reason to bring this guard back to Deck-D now is to get his Dog Tags. To do so, you must put the other two guards to sleep. After tranquilizing the corridor guard, drag him into the Mess Hall far enough so that the door will close. Then go into the pantry and stand on the south side of the food shelf. Wait until the guard enters and takes a position on the opposite end of the shelf. When the guard is facing north, run over and capture him from the side. Then move in front of the guard and go into First Person View. The guard is hostile and he will taunt you. If you stand there long enough, he will attempt to overthrow Snake! To show him you mean business, you must switch over to the USP and fire a warning shot close to his head. If that doesn't faze him, then shoot him in the hand or the shoulder. At that point, he'll gladly fork over the Dog Tags.

U.S.S. DISCOVERY: DECK-C

A new guard patrols the entire corridor on Deck-C. When Snake enters the area, the guard moves from the starboard to the port side, under the surveillance camera. This guard isn't hard to take down, just be careful of *when* you do it.

Deck-C Tactics

Deck-C Guard

The inept guard patrols back and forth down the corridor, never examining the large space under the stairs. Snake can hide from the guard in plain sight just by standing in this space.

Deck-C Guard

The guard immediately moves under the surveillance camera. Do not tranquilize the guard until he moves *past* the camera's cone of vision. If the camera watches the guard fall from a tranquilizer dart, it will know something is wrong and the alert will sound. After the guard is safely slumbering, it is possible to shoot out the camera with the USP if you desire.

DOG TAGS: Deck-C Guard

Difficulty: Very Easy

This guard is begging for Snake to get the drop on him, since he never looks toward the locker area. Wait by the port wall until the guard moves toward the starboard. The guard will pause just outside the starboard section of the corridor. Run up behind him and capture him for his Dog Tags. If the camera is still active, use a tranquilizer so that the sound isn't heard elsewhere.

U.S.S. DISCOVERY: DECK-B

The last time you came through here, we emphasized getting the guard's Dog Tags, so we will proceed to describe only how to obtain the **USP Bullets** from the south locker. By this point, you should be confident enough to subdue the guards in these simple corridors on your own.

Deck-B Tactics

Deck-B
Rear Hallway Guard

You've dealt with the guard who patrols in front of this locker before, so a general takedown should be sufficient.

--- STRATEGY ---

Deck-B Rear Hallway Guard

Move south from the port side entrance and press Snake's back against the southwest corner. When the guard moves back toward the locker, jump out and aim your dart at the base of his skull. As the guard falls, move down and collect the **USP Bullets** from the locker. Then stuff the guard's body in the locker just for fun.

U.S.S. DISCOVERY: DECK-A CREW'S LOUNGE

As you approach the lounge from the top of the central stairs, a lone guard patrols the area. He searches from port to starboard, so he is somewhat tricky to evade. The sleeping guard swarmed with flies in the starboard stairwell is hardly protecting the **USP Bullets** behind him. Snake could easily sneak in, get the bullets and sneak out, but that's hardly any *fun*, is it?

Deck-A Tactics

Crew's Lounge Guard

598010567300110400

Remain standing at the top of the stairs, out of the guard's sight. It is time to strike when the guard stands at either end of the lounge.

--- STRATEGY ---

Deck-A Crew's Lounge Guard

When the guard passes by, quickly descend the stairs and get into the right alcove under the stairs. Equip the M9 and shoot a hole in the glass pane, a few yards down. When the guard returns through the area, he will notice the hole and move to investigate. At this point, you can either get the drop on the guard for Dog Tags if you haven't done so already, or you can take a clear shot at a stationary target.

Port Stairwell Guard

The flies swarming around this drowsing guard should indicate something about his character. He is a surly mutt; handle him with extreme caution.

Deck-A Port Stairwell Guard

Sneak down the steps by pressing lightly on the Left Analog Stick. Clear Snake's hands of any weapons, and then move directly behind the guard. Press the ⬤ button to make Snake grab the guard in a chokehold. You can keep him like this until the guard passes out, or tap the ⬤ button rapidly to snap his neck like a twig. Then grab the bullets nearby.

DOG TAGS: Deck-A Port Stairwell Guard

Difficulty: Medium

Sneaking up behind the dozing guard and surprising him is relatively simple. But when you move in front of the guard and aim your weapon at his head, he will taunt you rather than beg for mercy. Be certain that all other guards in the area are knocked out first, equip the USP, and fire a warning shot over the guard's shoulder. If that doesn't convince him, shoot him in the hand or the shoulder to get the tags.

U.S.S. DISCOVERY: ENGINE ROOM

Knowing that visibility is a problem in the Engine Room, the terrorists have positioned guards at every level of the area. Crossing this zone will be a true test of Snake's infiltration abilities.

▦	**Ration**
USP	**USP Ammo**
🪖	**Grenades**

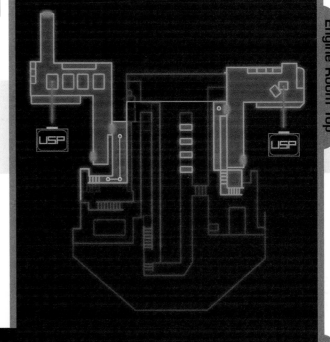

Engine Room Top

Engine Room Middle

Engine Room Bottom

Engine Room Reconnaissance

To reach the Engine Room, move to the starboard stairwell of the Deck-A Crew's Lounge and descend. Enter the door and move up the corridor. Snake spots a very intimidating shadow on the wall. Immediately call Otacon on the Codec, who recognizes it too. It's Vulcan Raven, back from the dead! He was the giant and shaman who worked as chief hunter and trap engineer for FOXHOUND during the Shadow Moses incident. Equip the M9 and jump out from the corner—only to find the true source of the shadow—it's the McFarlane Toys Vulcan Raven action figure! Kill the light source by firing a dart at the flashlight. You can activate the figure by shooting it. Vulcan will begin grunting and shooting pellets all over the room. You can knock the figure over by hitting it with darts, but it cannot be turned off. Take a photo of the Vulcan Raven figure with the Camera. If Snake says "Good," then Otacon will make comments later.

In the same room, hop onto the nearby crate to collect more **USP Bullets**. Open the locker on the far left, and a body falls out! Put it back inside to avoid suspicion. Proceed to the starboard entrance to the Engine Room, noting that there is a guard on the other side of the door.

In Normal Mode, there are six guards in the Engine Room. You must reach the small room on the upper-port side, so you need to use a lot of different strategies to get through the area without detection. You need to take out the guards quietly—there's no avoiding it here.

Running out of ammo in this area is hard to do. Use the maps provided to locate various ammo boxes and the **Ration**. There are **Grenades** at the bottom-left corner of the port side's lowest level. Whatever you do, don't miss out on these because they are extremely helpful in later events.

Navigate to the top level of the port side and enter the small room. Proceeding north in the hallway, a guard forces open the previously locked port side door. Quickly move into the open locker and seal Snake inside. Press R1 to look out through the vents, but be gentle or Snake will bang his head on the door and alert the guard. As you're holding R1, press R2 or L2 to look from side to side. When the guard stops outside the locker, he will look north for a moment and then head back down the south corridor. Exit the locker and continue moving on. **USP Bullets** sit on top of a small device.

IR sensor beam traps protect the watertight door in this small room. If you run through them, the detonation of the explosives will destroy the whole ship. You must deactivate three IR beam arrays by destroying the control boxes with the USP. If you miss and shoot the C4, you're toast.

Engine Room Tactics

Getting through six soldiers in one area is tough, but Snake has been out in the cold so long that the challenge is welcome. Each guard requires a different strategy, and taking out those IR beam control boxes isn't going to be easy either.

Engine Room Top Level, Starboard Guard

Standing just inside the starboard side door, this lazy guard rarely follows his patrol route and does a lot of stretching and yawning instead. He's begging for Snake to step up and tranquilize him, but obtaining the guard's Dog Tags isn't as simple as it seems...

---- STRATEGY ----

Top Level Starboard Guard

Easy—step up to the starboard door so that it opens, use First Person View, and place a dart at the base of the stationary guard's skull. Then drag him outside the mechanical area and stow him in the open locker. This way, he will remain asleep and will not return to his patrol route later.

DOG TAGS: Top Level Starboard Guard

Difficulty: Easy

Getting the drop on this guy is simple. But the problem is that he stands at the rail for long periods. If you capture him from inside the door, how will you position Snake in front of the guard? It is possible, but it's not always easy. An alternate way to capture him is to wait near the lockers in the room outside until the guard resumes his route and moves south. Then charge out the door, run down the platform after him, and try to get the drop before he turns around and spots you.

Engine Room **Middle Level**, Starboard Guard

The guard on the middle level patrols fastidiously north to south, pausing to look out over the lower rail. To reach the mid-level stairs, you need to take out this guard...

STRATEGY

Middle Level Starboard Guard

There are two ways to get this guy. To put him to sleep, move to the south of the upper level and crouch. When the guard moves to the south corner of the middle level, fire a dart into the back of his skull. Also, Snake can drop on this guard and knock him out. From the top level, drop over the rail and hang. Use First Person View to look down and aim. As the guard walks under Snake, press ⊗ to drop onto the guard and knock him out. However, the effect lasts only as long as the stars swirl around the guard's head.

DOG TAGS: Middle Level Starboard Guard

Difficulty: Medium

Getting the drop on this guard requires that Snake does a little dropping of his own. As the guard is moving from the north part of his route to the south, jump over the top level's rail and hang. When the guard passes underneath, drop behind him and press ● to surprise him. Hopefully, you'll reach the guard before he gets to the rail, or there won't be any room to get in front of him.

Engine Room **Lower Level**, Starboard Guard

This guard stands in a stationary position in a small alcove at the bottom of the stairs. It is very easy for this guard to spot intruders approaching from the port side, but otherwise he's easy to take out.

STRATEGY

Lower Level Starboard Guard

The stationary position of this guard makes him very easy to take out from two directions. Here's an interesting way to do it. Move to the southeast corner of the middle level. Jump over the rail at the small corner and drop to the floor. Press Snake's back against the corner, then press ● to jump out. Then use First Person View to carefully aim a shot at the guard's head.

DOG TAGS: Lower Level Starboard Guard

Difficulty: Very Easy

Ease down the stairs behind the guard. Stay behind the corner until the stationary soldier looks the other way. Press ● to jump out from the corner, and Snake will easily get the drop on him. Gently lower your gun, then get in front of him and coerce the Dog Tags from him.

0151937100

Engine Room Middle Level, Central Guard

A guard stands at the south end of the middle platform, staring out over the abyss with his scope. Do not cross the area under this guard unless you see in the Soliton Radar screen that the guard is using his binoculars.

STRATEGY

Middle Level Central Guard

Since the guard spends most of his time surveying the south area, he is quite easy to sneak up behind and overtake. The only real trick is to avoid getting spotted by him when you cross under his location. When the soldier looks through his binoculars, his cone of vision on the Soliton Radar map becomes much longer and narrower.

DOG TAGS: Middle Level Central Guard

Difficulty: Hard

Wait to try for this guard's Dog Tags until all the other guards in the room are tranquilized. Getting close to this guard isn't difficult, and capturing him is a cinch. Just avoid being seen as you cross under his area on the level below, and you'll capture this guard. However, once you get in front of him, the guard becomes defiant and challenges you! You must equip the USP and fire a warning shot or two close to his head. If that doesn't do it, shoot him in the arm and he will hand over his tags. Firing those shots will alert other guards who are active in the area, so make this guy your last target if you want his tags.

Engine Room Lower Level, Port Side Guard

Patrolling a very tight area of the lower level on the port side, this sentry guards a box of **USP Bullets** sitting nearby, and he guards them well. If you need those bullets, you can take down this guard from long range.

STRATEGY

Lower Level Port Side Guard

Approaching this guard is difficult. The best way to take him down is to move across the middle level to the stairs on the south part of the port side. From the bottom of the stairs, carefully aim down the narrow walkway and use First Person View to hit the guard in the head with a tranquilizer. If the first shot misses or causes the guard to investigate, aim and fire another dart as he approaches your position. You should have plenty of time to knock him out before he reaches Snake's location at the bottom of the walkway.

```
10240132
01478
```

DOG TAGS: Lower Level Port Side Guard

Difficulty: Very Hard

How do you get a drop on a guard who patrols swiftly and has good visibility in all directions? Move across the middle level to the rail above the guard's position. Watch his cone of vision carefully on the Soliton Radar. He will search the area to the south, under where you are standing. The instant he turns north, jump over the rail and drop to the floor below. Run two or three steps toward the guard and press ○ quickly! Then run *through* the guard to the side he is facing and quickly aim at him again before he runs off. This desperate strategy can work, and it's sure to get your adrenaline rushing!

Engine Room Top Level, Port Side Guard

The guard nearest Snake's destination is easier to take out with a tranquilizer fired at long range from the opposite side of the room. If you can't make the shot from there, then close quarters tactics are required.

STRATEGY

Top Level Port Side Guard

Move up the stairs to the small, dark alcove just below the top platform. Watch the guard's pattern on the Soliton for a moment. After the guard stares for a moment down the stairs where you are hiding, carefully sneak up behind him by pressing lightly on the Left Analog Stick.

DOG TAGS: Top Level Port Side Guard

Difficulty: Easy

Follow the tactic described above, except wait for the guard to turn away from the rail and head north toward the exit. Then run up the stairs and get the drop on him before he gets too far away. This way, you can freeze him when he is not facing the rail. This provides room to move Snake in front of the guard.

Engine Room Turbine Area Guard

When Snake enters the small turbine area and proceeds north, a guard will unseal the door behind him and enter. When he radios in, the sentry announces that he's about to patrol the area!

STRATEGY

Turbine Area Guard

Quickly move to the open locker near the IR beams in the back corner and seal Snake inside. From here, you can see through the vent holes as the guard approaches. Outside the locker, the guard will turn to examine the IR beams before heading south and out of the area. The safest thing to do here is just avoid conflict by hiding from the guard.

DOG TAGS: Turbine Area Guard

Difficulty: Medium

Follow the strategy described previously. When the guard turns and heads south from in front of the locker, step out and follow the guard to his stopping point in the southeast corner. There, you can catch up to him and surprise him for his tags.

200159801

Engine Room IR Beams C4 Trap

Equip the Thermal Goggles so Snake can see the beams crisscrossing the corridor. Destroying the three control boxes that power the beams will deactivate them.

Engine Room IR Beam C4 Trap

The control boxes for the beams are snuggled away in tight spots. Two of them require that you shoot over C4 bricks, which means that your aiming in First Person View must be sharp. Hop onto the turbine, where you can obtain **USP Bullets**, and take a Pentazemin pill to steady your shots. Equip the Thermal Goggles, and the control boxes will stand out from the rest of the surroundings.

For the uppermost control box, stand on the turbine and look down the right side of the passage. A control box sits high up, behind a C4 patch. To have a better shot at it, stand on Snake's tiptoes by holding R2 and L2 while still holding R1 . Aim at the top part of the control box to avoid hitting the explosives. This will disengage the first set of IR beams.

After the first beams are down, keep the Thermal Goggles on and hop off the turbine. Move a little ways down the corridor and look down to the right. The control box for the second IR beam array rests on the floor; you just have to get closer to improve your chances of hitting it. This deactivates the second set of beams.

Move as far into the hall as possible. Then crouch and lay Snake flat on the floor, facing the watertight door. With the Thermal Goggles equipped, look to the left side of the passage in First Person View. The last control box is wedged between two C4 packs, and your shot needs to be darned accurate. Take another Pentazemin if it's hard to aim steadily. This should disengage the final IR beam array.

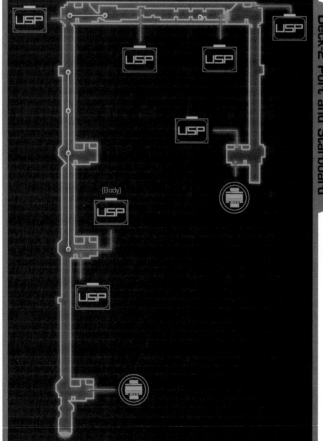

DECK-2, PORT

Deck-2 Port and Starboard

A general announcement orders the Marines to report to the hold in 10 minutes for the Commandant's speech. Snake must navigate through these narrow passages in order to reach the tanker's central cargo holds.

	Ration
USP	**USP Ammo**

9 7 0 0 1 2 3 6

Deck-2 RECONnaissance

Lights Out

Lighting is the problem here. Guards in these corridors can see a remarkable distance away, especially when you're standing in a well-lit area. Use the USP to shoot out the light bulbs hanging above the doorways. Check carefully because the electric breakers in this area are jittery and some light bulbs turn on intermittently. Play it safe and shoot every light bulb you can, whether it is illuminated or not.

You'll find that blasting out the light in the first alcove makes this section of the corridor much darker. Grab the **Ration** and continue north—the watertight door here is sealed.

You should halt in the passage before you arrive at the second alcove. From here, shoot out light bulbs that are further down the passage. Use First Person View to aim at the tiny dots of light, then use the Scope to confirm that you blasted them all. Occasionally put on the Thermal Goggles, which will help you spot approaching soldiers.

The watertight door in the second alcove is also sealed. There are **USP Bullets**, and if you shake down the dead crewmember here, he will drop some more. Drag the body into the alcove so you can engage the south corridor guard in some espionage tactics.

Moving north from the second alcove will trigger a guard to follow his patrol route, which extends just past the second alcove. This is a good time for Snake to take down this guard and move on.

Avoiding Unwelcome Attention

Remember that the flashlight on the USP will alert nearby guards, so switch back to the M9 whenever you have tranquilizing to do.

More lit areas should come into view as you approach the northern end of the corridor. Shoot out the lights from as far away as possible, including the one above the watertight door at the end. A guard listening to music will arrive as you reach the corner. Take down this guard quietly, because another soldier is just yards away. There are **USP Bullets** at the corner to help keep you stocked.

Moving east, it's important *not* to shoot out the lights anymore. The sound of smashing bulbs will alert the guard who is dozing between his reports. Carefully sneak up on him between each of his drowsy calls in, and attack him from close range. There are more **USP Bullets** near this soldier, and another box sits by the watertight door that leads to the east corridor.

Deck-2 Port Tactics

Use the tips mentioned earlier to navigate down the corridor. Knock out lights from as far away as possible. When it comes to confronting guards, utilize the following strategies to break through.

Deck-2, North-South Patrolling Guard

Keep a sharp eye out for this long-roaming guard. Equip the Thermal Goggles as you approach the second alcove to easily spot the sentry advancing.

STRATEGY

North-South Patrolling Guard Tactic

As the guard approaches, there is plenty of time to line up a tranquilizer shot in First Person View. Avoid using the USP, since even at some distance the guard will spot the flashlight attached to the barrel. Keep the Thermal Goggles equipped to see better in the dark you've created. Since the IR negates the laser sighting, line up the M9 barrel with the guard's head.

DOG TAGS: North-South Patrolling Guard

Difficulty: Easy

When you move toward the second alcove, the guard is triggered to begin his southbound patrol. Use the Thermal Goggles to spot him coming. Make sure you drag the dead crewmember out of the way, since Snake has a tendency to move slowly over dead bodies.

Hide behind the small corner in the alcove, and watch the soldier's approach on the Soliton. When the guard moves past the alcove, he will pause just beyond your position. This is the time to come out of the alcove and surprise him.

Deck-2, Jamming Guard

Although this guard's hearing is compromised by his headphones, his visual acuity is still sharp. When he moves to the northwest corner, he will pause for a long, vulnerable moment.

STRATEGY

Jamming Guard Tactic

Approaching the northwest corner of the corridor, keep a sharp eye on the Soliton Radar. The guard boogies into view, engrossed in his tunes. You should be able to hear the music he listens to from some distance away. Stand just outside the corner area, and aim a tranquilizer at the guard's neck in First Person View. Drag the body south out of the corner area, so that the last guard doesn't spot the body for any reason.

DOG TAGS: Jamming Guard

Difficulty: Very Easy

When the guard stops at the corner and is facing west, simply run up from the side and capture him. There is still plenty of room for Snake to get in front of the guard and harass him for his Dog Tags. Do not try to capture the guard if he is facing east, or the other guard dozing nearby might see you. After you tranquilize the musical guard, drag him south, so that Snake's further movement east is not compromised.

Deck-2, Sleep-Talking Soldier

This guard is so dedicated to the rebirth of Mother Russia, that he reports to his superiors even in his sleep. Taking him out is going to be a challenge, though, since he occasionally awakens and looks around.

STRATEGY

Sleep-Talking Soldier Tactic

Don't shoot out any more lights, or the sound of breaking glass will alert the guard. Wait for him to report in, then move through the next section and hide behind the left corner before the next report. Once the guard reports in again, you can to jump out from the corner and enter First Person View to target his neck. After you tranquilize this guard, Snake should leave this area before the commander gets worried and dispatches another team to investigate.

DOG TAGS: Sleep-Talking Guard

Difficulty: Very Hard

Move to the corridor section that precedes the guard's position, and hide against the south wall. Watch him for a while on the radar. Notice the pattern in which his cone of vision comes and goes. As soon as he closes his eyes, jump out and surprise him with the M9. The problem is that, although the guard's cone of vision disappears, his eyes are still half-open and he may spot Snake before he can yell "Freeze!"

DECK-2, STARBOARD

Deck-2 Starboard Reconnaissance

It's Quiet—Too Quiet

The second section of corridor that runs around the outside of the Holds area is empty and quiet; this is a bad sign. Equip Snake's Rations, and resume shooting out lights in this corridor—you'll need as much darkness as possible.

There are some **USP Bullets** in a well-lit area at the first corner. You should definitely shoot out all of the lights here. Move down to the first alcove. From here, use First Person View to look as far south down the corridor as possible and shoot out all the lights you can. The firefight you're about to enter demands that you hide well in the dark. After you've taken out as many lights as you can, grab the **USP Bullets** and **Ration** in the alcove and continue south. A short cut scene begins.

Deck-2 Starboard Tactics

Three guards enter and a firefight between Snake and the soldiers breaks out in the hallway. More guards will pour into the alcove after you defeat the first wave, and even more after that will charge at Snake.

8 7 0 2 0 0 1 5 9 8 0 1 0 1 0 0 2 1 4 0 0 3 8 7

4 0 0 1 1 0

Corridor Standoff Tactics

Equip the Grenades and quickly move forward to the crate that is closest to the intersection. Crouch behind the crate and press Snake's back up against it. When the soldiers disappear out of view for a moment, hold L2 so that Snake peaks around the crate, then press ⬤ hard for a second and release. Snake will throw a Grenade into the intersection and take out the first wave of guards.

Now equip the USP and press yourself against the crate again. Jump out and enter First Person View. When the single guard behind the crate on the other side of the intersection rises up, fill him full of lead. If you miss him, the guard will throw a Grenade of his own to flush out Snake. This causes heavy damage if the grenade is successful. The second wave of troops should be in the intersection by now, so keep the USP handy and use jump-out shots to nail them when they step into view.

After the soldier behind the crate is dead, leave the crate and run north. You should find two boxes of **USP Bullets** and a **Ration**. As you're standing here, a squad of three troopers will charge at you. Since they have to thin out to get around the crates, start blasting with the USP and you'll kill them one by one.

After the smoke clears, Snake enters the Holds area, where Metal Gear RAY is kept. No wonder Snake is a legend—he has almost completed his mission!

CARGO HOLDS
1, 2, and 3
Cargo Holds Reconnaissance

Snake stands on a balcony high above a crowd of soldiers. The holds are being used as a makeshift stadium where the Marine Commandant is giving his speech.

Otacon explains the situation. The tanker's holds are divided into three sections, and RAY is in the furthest hold. Snake must head north through rooms full of Marines watching the speech.

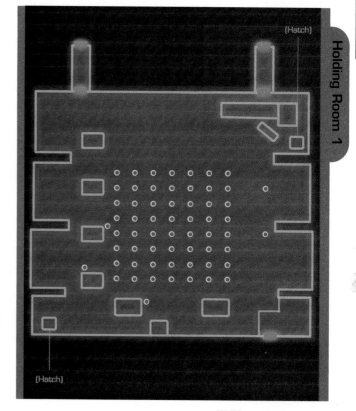

Holding Room 1

(Hatch)

(Hatch)

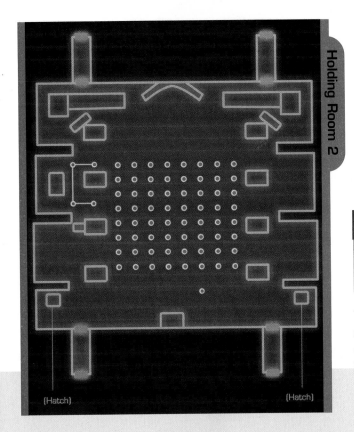

(Hatch)   (Hatch)

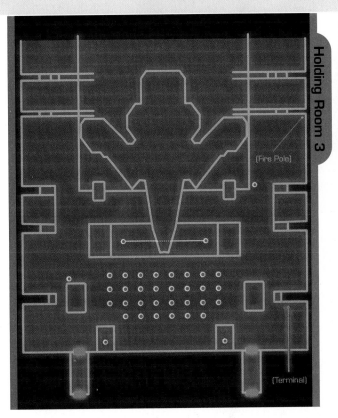

(Fire Pole)

(Terminal)

Game Over, Man!

If Snake is spotted, he will be arrested and the game will end instantly.

The Commandant's speech lasts exactly seven minutes. Snake must get the photos of RAY before the speech ends, or the soldiers will return to their posts. You can hear the speech in the background as you work. Your mission objective is to capture four photos of Metal Gear RAY: three angles from the front and a fourth shot of the "MARINE" lettering somewhere on the mech.

Metal Gear Theater

The broadcast of the General's speech is a stunning event, with great direction and presentation. Sometime when you're replaying the game just for fun, stop and watch the entire speech on one of the large projection screens—it will almost certainly fill you with American pride!

Above and Below...

On the next page, you'll find our strategies for negotiating through the main floors of the three cargo holds. However, this is not the only path available to you. Investigate these large rooms to find alternate paths, both below the main floor *and* above. This might be a good time to start leveling up your Grip Gauge...

Cargo Holds Tactics

Hold No. 1 Tactics

Descend the two ladders to the floor. From your position at the back of the room, the screen that the soldiers are watching is situated at the far end on the right, so you'll have to navigate along the back wall and the left side of the room to get through here. Go ahead and run normally to the left until you reach the projector, then crouch and crawl under the front of it. Be careful not to crawl in front of the guard standing just below the projector, and continue along the back wall.

There is another ladder at the bottom of the west wall. Snake can climb up and find a box of **M9 Bullets** at the top, but it's not worth the time for reasons that will become all too clear very quickly.

and air background.

Continue along the west wall, and be careful of iron grates in the floor. If Snake runs over them at normal speed, the clatter will cause the closest Marine to investigate. Sneak across floor grates by lightly pressing the Left Analog Stick. Then exit through the door to the next hold.

will think twice about their nuclear strategy

Hold No. 2 Tactics

Inside the second hold, take a quick look to the north in First Person View. Crates and other obstructions block the western path. Even if you can get around the crates, a Marine is patrolling on the other side of them.

I know that is my duty.

The safest route is to move east along the back wall, and then north along the east wall. As you approach the twin projectors, something interesting will happen. The projectors are alternating in this hold, so that the speech is being shown alternately on two screens. The Marines' cones of view shift back and forth so that they intermittently stare at the east wall!

Move toward the projectors, then crouch and crawl under their beams. Once Snake is safely past the projectors, stand and move behind the first large object on the east side of the room. There are floor grates behind each of these hiding spots, so Snake must sneak or crawl across them. Wait for the projectors to switch to the west screen, and try to make your way up the eastern side as quickly as possible without making any noise.

and the program was already attracting strong criticism

Depending on your timing so far, the Commandant may take a break in his speech. He will lead the Marines through a series of neck stretches. The Marines will be looking up and down, left and right. Find a hiding spot and stay put the whole time this is going on. When the Commandant resumes his speech, continue to the north end of the room.

Navigate Snake quietly around the large speakers and the media equipment piled up at the north end. The door is situated behind these obstacles.

of the Anti-Ballistic Missile agreement.

Hold No. 3 Tactics

Solid Snake finally reaches the hold where his long-time nemesis is on display. Although Metal Gear is just a weapon employed by mankind, the various mechanical prototypes that Snake has fought during the course of his career still seem to have an ominous quality. For Snake, Metal Gear is the root of all evil. He once again stands before a new Metal Gear.

Marine Commandant General Scott Dolph stands on the platform erected in front of the new prototype. The men in this room give him their undivided attention. Crewmembers on platforms to the left and right are filming this auspicious event, so their attention is also focused. Snake should have very little trouble completing the task at hand.

Previous Photo Critique Time

The console where Snake needs to upload the shots is situated near the entrance on the east side of the room. If you've taken shots of pinup girls, unconscious Olga, or the Vulcan Raven Action Figure with the Camera, go ahead and try an upload. Otacon's responses to these shots are quite amusing!

Duplicate this shot for best results.

The Front-Right Photo: Otacon reminds Snake of what pictures to capture. After the scene and the Codec conversation, Snake is stands in the perfect spot from which to capture the "front-right" photo. Simply equip the Camera, frame as much of RAY in the shot as possible, and press ● to shoot. We've provided decent example photos that will get you through this part of the game if you can duplicate them.

The Front-Center Photo: After taking the front-right shot, sneak around the base of the platform where the camera-man stands and move to the south wall, near the black centerline on the floor. Equip the camera and try to frame as much of RAY as possible in the shot. This is your "front-center" shot.

Duplicate this shot for best results.

Expert Photography

Snake may make a comment after you take a shot. If Snake says "Good," then the photo will satisfy the mission requirements. If Snake says "Alright!" then the photo will receive the best possible response from Otacon after you upload the shots.

Duplicate this shot for best results.

Continue sneaking to the left, staying close under the platform where the second camera-man is stationed. Position Snake near the front-left corner of the technician's platform, equip the camera and frame your shot. It's okay if the walkway sticks out in front of RAY's "face" a little bit. The shot will get a better rating from Otacon if you crouch so that RAY's "face" can be seen better under the walkway.

From there, sneak north past the lone guard on the side. We recommend crawling behind the guard, just to be safe. Continue along the west wall to the end, and aim the camera at RAY. Here, you should be able to see the "MARINES" lettering on the side of the mechanical beast. Don't zoom in on it too closely; Otacon wants to see that the lettering is actually a part of RAY.

Duplicate this shot for best results.

False Alarm

At roughly two minutes left to go in the speech, the general will suddenly shout, "Intruder on the Left! Intruder on the right!" Although you hear the alerts, don't sweat it. The General is only drilling his men. However, if you are unlucky enough to be in the open when the men respond to the General, your mission could end right there.

If time runs out, don't panic. The General, loving to hear himself talk, will go on! So, the timing of the speech is not your worst problem—just concentrate on sneaking carefully and getting the photos.

Now return to the command console on the east side of the room, near the entrance, and press ▲ to upload the pics. Otacon will critique them. He will accept photos where you framed as much of RAY as possible in the shot. The "MARINE" lettering is a must for Otacon, so he will send you back if you don't have the shot exactly as he wants it. If he doesn't like one of the angle photos, or maybe two of them, the game will still continue. If Otacon deems all four shots worthless, then he'll send you back to redo them.

the future of the country

You're a pretty good photographer. We can definitely use this left shot.

General Scott Dolph

General Dolph has worked hard and fought bravely all throughout his military career, believing in the causes of the American people and its government. His inspiring leadership skills make him the perfect commandant to martial the U.S. Marines forces. Though divorced for many years, his beliefs have not faltered and he continues to struggle for peace and prosperity in the world. His personal goal in life is that his troubled daughter might finally see that mankind lives in a peace-loving world, where everyone is safe. The general views the rise of Metal Gear programs around the world as the most powerful threat to freedom that has ever existed. In the past two years, he has worked hard with military intelligence to create the first prototype of a Marine anti-terrorist amphibious battle tank. RAY is a Metal Gear for fighting other Metal Gears. This project represents the culmination of Commandant Dolph's life work.

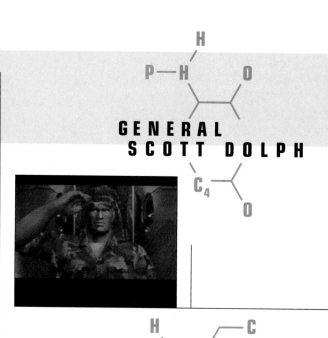

GENERAL SCOTT DOLPH

COLONEL SERGEI GURLUKOVICH

Colonel Sergei Gurlukovich

The Colonel is the leader of a private Russian military army he assembled following the end of the Cold War. Manpower was easy to come by when thousands of former Soviet soldiers and KGB agents suddenly found themselves unemployed in the late 1980s. The goal of his organization is to restore military power and dignity to Mother Russia, Gurlukovich's self-styled ideal of a military-controlled utopia in the former communist nation.

REVOLVER OCELOT

11010

G O H₃

Shalashaska, a.k.a. "Revolver" Ocelot

A well known terrorist from the Shadow Moses Incident two years ago, "Revolver" is the Russian double agent who stole the exercise data of the Metal Gear REX combat test, and sold the specifications for the weapon on the international black market. His two names indicate more than just the duplicity of his nature, each also represents a different aspect of his personality. "Revolver" is an expert marksman with superhuman quick-draw skills and a love of old-time American cowboy films. There is no man who handles a pair of six shooters better. As for "Shalashaska," the prisoners of Russia bestowed this name upon him while he was working as an interrogation methods consultant to the Soviet Spetsnaz during the Cold War. A brutal and highly intelligent former FOXHOUND agent, Ocelot's cunning is a perfect match for Solid Snake's razor sharp survival skills. But as we soon witness, there seems to be another factor currently affecting Ocelot's behavior...

MISSION ANALYSIS—PLANT

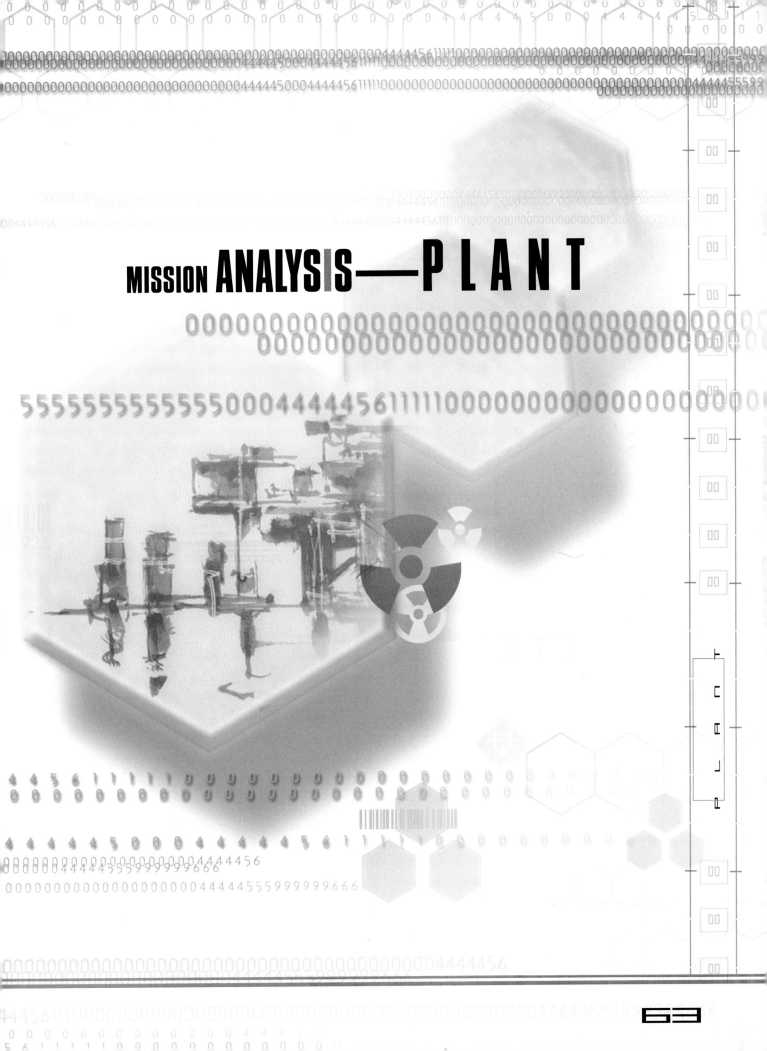

2 part MISSION ANALYSIS

PLANT

Offshore decontamination facility "Big Shell"

Come in from downwind, then pull up fast!

A VIP from one of the major conservation groups,

The Big Shell is the massive environmental containment unit built in New York's Hudson Bay to prevent ecological contamination due to the massive spread of crude oil spilled during the sinking of the U.S.S. Discovery two years ago. Six hours ago, the Big Shell was seized by former members of the Navy SEALS special anti-terrorist training squad "Dead Cell," in cooperation with a well-armed private Russian army. They have thirty or more civilian hostages, including United States President James Johnson. The hijackers are demanding thirty billion dollars in ransom. If their demands are not met, the terrorists plan to demolish the Big Shell with explosives. Navy unit SEAL Team 10 has been dispatched to invade the Big Shell, landing on the heliport pads of the facility. In a covert backup effort, an operative of the FOXHOUND special forces unit has been inserted into the Big Shell via underwater infiltration. Snake swims into the Deep Sea Dock.

Strut A:
DEEP SEA DOCK

Change of Format

Whereas the Tanker portion of the Mission Analysis was divided into the major areas of the U.S.S. Discovery, coverage of the Big Shell facility is handled in a mission-based fashion. You will often move between multiple areas, sometimes revisiting specific sections more than once, as you work toward achieving your objectives. Therefore, the focus is on the major tasks, rather than confining coverage to specific areas.

Chief of Operations

140.85

COLONEL

Colonel Campbell will provide information on Snake's mission objectives, which is helpful if you just booted up the game from a save file. He will explain all of the functions of the controller, as well as basic stealth and combat tactics. Campbell is also capable of providing background information on the structure of the Big Shell and profiles on the key players in this operation.

"Dead Cell"

Dead Cell is a highly skilled anti-terrorist training squad developed under the Navy SEALS with the guidance of former U.S. President George Sears. Their purpose was to stage random terrorist simulations to test the countermeasures of the SEALS and other military branches. Six months ago, all of that changed when former Dead Cell leader Colonel Jackson was arrested on charges of corruption and misappropriation of funds. It was a devastating event for the group, and apparently they snapped. They began attacking various military installations as well as federal office buildings. They are as ruthless as the terrorists they were trained to emulate, and their knowledge of military anti-terrorist response measures makes Dead Cell a formidable enemy.

The name was originally intended to reflect its anti-terrorist functions.

SOLIDUS
SNAKE

VAMP

FORTUNE

FATMAN

N—O   H—OH
RAIDEN
O   CH₃

The rookie operative codenamed "Raiden" is an unseasoned veteran of over 300 VR missions, plus the full simulations of Shadow Moses, Zanzibar, and Outer Heaven. While fully trained in the required abilities of a FOXHOUND agent, he has never tasted true battle. However, the comfort he displays in the field indicates that this young man has a bright future in the shadow services, and he may one day even fill the gigantic shoes of the legendary Solid Snake. Under the guidance of Snake's former ally and personal friend, Colonel Roy Campbell, Raiden is sure to liberate the Big Shell from the evil clutches of Dead Cell. He just needs to settle things with his girlfriend, Rose, who acts as mission analyst and can't seem to get the hang of referring to him by his designated codename.

9001750 34   08415

01398010100217 00397

1   0   02006

MISSION 01: RECONNAISSANCE

After a quick consultation with Colonel Roy Campbell, commander of this operation, your FOXHOUND operative codename is switched to "Raiden." The Colonel will call several times while you examine the hangar. He'll advise you on basic operations and item usage.

Having infiltrated the Deep Sea Dock at the bottom of the Big Shell's Strut A, the first objective is to get up to the surface of Strut A. There is an elevator to the surface at the north end of the docks area.

Strut A: Deep Sea Dock

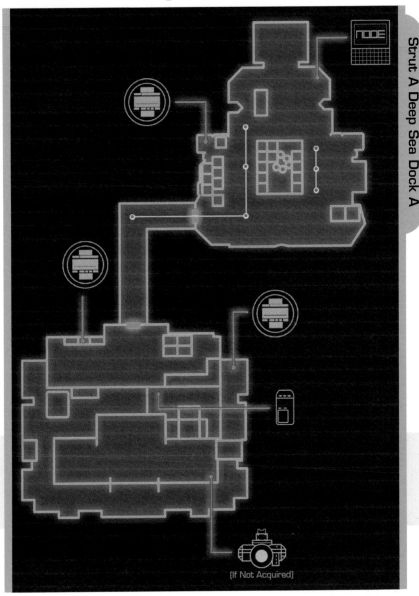

Strut A Deep Sea Dock A

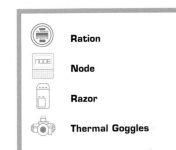

🔲	Ration
NODE	Node
🔲	Razor
🔲	Thermal Goggles

(If Not Acquired)

There are several things to do in the Deep Sea Dock that are a little outside the mission. From the starting position, switch to First Person View and turn around and look at the wall crawling with bugs, then call the Colonel for information on them. If Raiden crawls through these bugs, there is a danger that they will get on the Rations. Sea lice feed on food sources, and your Rations will slowly be reduced to zero if you don't do anything about them.

Shooing Away Sea Lice

If a red bug appears on the Rations icon in your left inventory menu, hold L2 and press up and down rapidly on the d-pad. This is called "shaking off" the bugs. If sea lice are left to feed on your Rations long enough, they'll leave you without any.

Swimming Controls

Dive into the water and press ◎ to submerge under the surface. Campbell will call immediately and provide instructions on how to swim. Swim to the lower southeast corner to find the submerged **Thermal Goggles**.

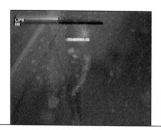

Surface and move to the ladder, then press △ to climb out.

Initial Supplies

If you crouch and crawl into the vent beside the stairs where the sea lice are crawling, you might get bugs on your Rations. Move to the western section of the room and use First Person View to find the vent leading under the platform from this side. Crawl straight through the vent to the other side of the room, where the water pressure tank sections off a small space. Here you will find a **Ration**. Colonel Campbell calls with some good tactical advice about using Rations during your mission.

In the lockers on the back wall, Raiden will find another **Ration** in the center locker. One more item to collect remains in the area, and it's partially hidden.

1 0 2 4 0 1 3 2 9 5 0 0 1 0 0 2 1 4 8 6 0 1 8
0 1 4 7 8 7 3 7 0 5 0 1 1

The Shaver

*Use First Person View to look into the cage with the large deep sea diving suits, and you'll notice a small item box marked "SHAVER" rotating in the corner. To reach this item, face the railing around the pool and press △ to jump over it and hang. Shimmy to the right and press △ again to jump into the small caged area and grab the item. When the **Shaver** is in your inventory, it will affect cinemas later in the game. You might want to play your first game without grabbing the Shaver, just so you can actually see what the changes are.*

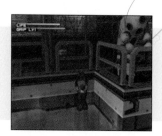

Trail of the Intruder

Open the watertight hatch at the top of the pool area. Raiden spots a sentry that has been attacked. The sentry leaves, so proceed quickly up the corridor and through the sliding door.

The guards in the cargo area have been knocked out cold. Raiden will have to wait until the platform elevator comes back down before he can go up.

Big Shell Nodes

Campbell explains the Soliton Radar system to Raiden. Each time Raiden enters a new floor level, he will have to download the map of the area from the local area Node. When you enter a new area and need to know the exact location of the Node, call Colonel Campbell. Campbell describes the locations pretty well, so don't spend a lot of time searching for Nodes without his help.

First Login

Proceed into the cargo warehouse area. Move up the west side of the room and hop onto the crates to collect another **Ration**.

Since the guards will be unconscious longer than usual, Raiden can shake down their bodies for useful items. Then move to the Node console on the right side of the elevator and login. Raiden is asked to enter a name.

Big Shell Map

After the login, you can view a full map of the Big Shell by pressing the START button. The names and functions of Shell 1 and its six Struts are displayed when you highlight them. Move the right analog stick to rotate the map.

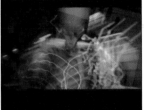

Identification Confirmed

The name and information you enter at the first Node will be seen again in a special way at the end of the game!

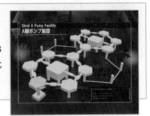

The Unexpected Guest

ROSE

Raiden's girlfriend Rose will act as mission analyst and record Jack's game data. Whenever you want to find out more about Raiden's past and his relationship with Rose, contact her and save your game.

Deep Sea Dock Tactics

After Raiden logs in, the guards will start to awaken. You should have enough time to run south in the room and hide amid the stacks of boxes on the middle pallet. The guards will radio an alert, and the whole place will go into Caution mode for a time. Don't panic; just stay low on the inside of the pallet and wait for the appropriate moment to move. The guard on the west side of the room will move into the corridor. This is the perfect opportunity to escape from your hiding spot on the pallet and make a break for the elevator. Just make sure that the guard on the east side of the room is not facing the elevator when you go for it, or your movement will draw his attention in this small, well-lit room.

Strut A: Pump Facility

Campbell explains that the President was sighted in Strut B, which isn't far away. After the Colonel signs off, call him again and he'll explain where the next Node is.

Roof Reconnaissance

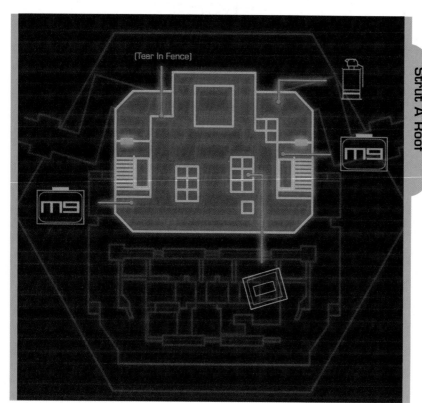

[Tear In Fence]

Strut A Roof

Bandage

M9 Ammo

Chaff Grenades

```
0 2 4 0 7 4 5
0 1 0 0 2 1 4 0 0 3 8 7
```

```
0 0 2 0 0 6 9
```

Move down from Raiden's position and hop onto the crates for a **Bandage**. There are **M9 Bullets** in the lower-left corner of the roof, but you'll need the appropriate gun to obtain them.

Move to the upper-left corner, where the Colonel contacts Raiden and points out the hole in the bottom of the fence. Crouch and crawl through the hole, and the Colonel will contact Raiden again with a status update on SEAL Team 10. Enter Strut A through the western door.

Poop Alert!

If Raiden runs over an area where there are bird droppings on the deck, he will slip and fall. Also, if Raiden stands in one place too long, one of the temperamental birds might drop a load on his head.

Strut A: Pump Room

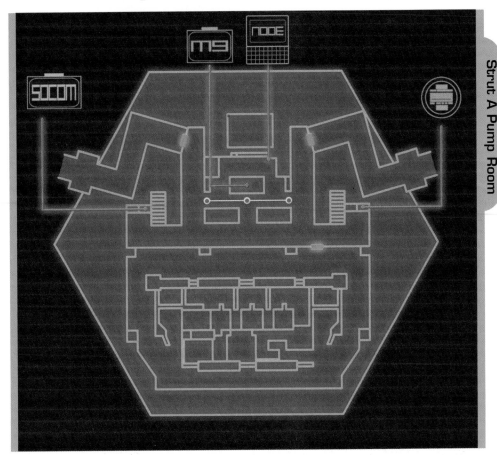

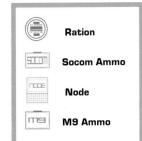

Legend:

Ration	
SOCOM	Socom Ammo
NODE	Node
M9	M9 Ammo

At the bottom of the stairs, two guards split up. Raiden can spot the location of the Node at the top of the area. Knocking on the partition wall can distract the guard patrolling this area. The best time to knock is when the guard is searching the west side of the room near the entrance to the AB Connector Bridge. As soon as the guard hears the noise, stop hugging the wall so that you can see the guard's movement direction in the top-down camera view. Run around the partition in the opposite direction, and sneak over to the Node to download the map of Strut A.

OSP (On-Site Procurement) in Strut A

As the guard returns to his position, hide behind the central desk. While you're there, crouch and look under the desk to spot a stash of **M9 Bullets**. Remember that they're here in case you need them later in the game.

There are other items hidden in the control room portion of the Pump Facility, some of which you can't collect until later. Under the west stairs, the right locker contains **Socom Bullets**. Leave the locker door open to remind you that they are there. The right locker under the east stairs holds a **Ration**. Another box of **M9 Bullets** is at the top of the stairs. You can obtain some **Chaff Grenades** if you run out to the Roof through this door. A guard patrols the roof, so get back inside quickly. Return to the cubicle area and sneak past the guard.

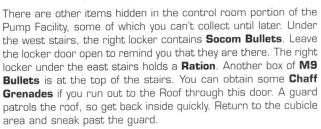

Brief Diversion

Raiden's current lack of a firearm is probably bothering you. Intelligence reports indicate that an M9 Tranquilizer Gun is located just inside the Strut F Warehouse, where it should be easy to obtain. To provide you with every possible advantage, this Mission Analysis will divert you to the warehouse briefly to obtain this weapon.

FA Connecting Bridge

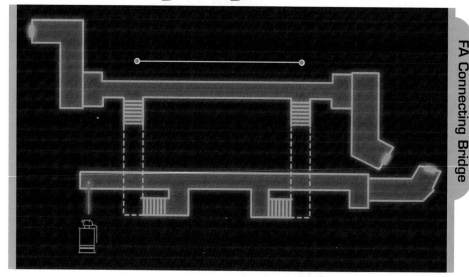

Chaff Grenade

Guards and/or automated sentries (Cyphers) monitor most of the connecting bridges between the struts. These bridges are treacherous areas because Raiden is out in the daylight and there are few places to hide. Guards can see further when there is plenty of light, so your objectives in these areas will be harder to accomplish. It's best to get across the bridges as quickly as possible without being spotted.

FA Bridge Tactics

When Raiden enters the FA Connecting Bridge area, Campbell contacts Raiden about the Cypher. This transmission includes a visual Codec tutorial on how to use Chaff Grenades against Cyphers. Also, notice how Raiden is shown throwing a grenade from behind a wall. This is a good strategy to master if you have the opportunity.

But you can use chaff to set up an interference field. That'll knock its sensors offline for a while.

There are two ways to get across the bridge. Either employ the Chaff Grenade method demonstrated by the Colonel, or just watch the floating device in First Person View until the Cypher moves below the sight line of the upper level. Either way, run down the first set of stairs on the bridge to the lower platform. The Cypher can't detect Raiden down here because of the pipes obstructing its view. Raiden can find **Chaff Grenades** on the closest side of the lower platform.

Cross the lower portion of the bridge, throwing a Chaff Grenade as you go. The Chaff disrupts the Cypher and lets Raiden enter Strut F. Make sure you enter the *upper* level—that's where the M9 is located.

Strut F **Warehouse**

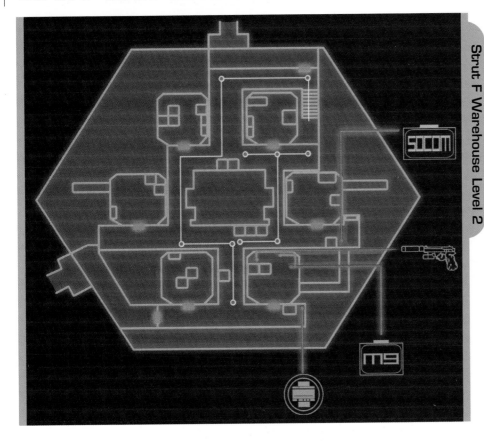

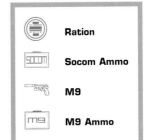

	**Ration**
	Socom Ammo
	M9
	M9 Ammo

Just inside the Warehouse, Raiden spots a guard on duty. The guard radios in every minute or so. If he fails to report, an investigation team will be dispatched. It is important to avoid tranquilizing or killing a guard that must report in. If you must take down a reporting guard for any reason, be prepared to leave the area when the security supervisor demands a status report over the radio. A second investigation team will be dispatched to find out the problem and wake up any sleeping guards.

Codec Chatter

140.85

COLONEL/ROSE

After Raiden watches the soldier report in, contact the Colonel. First, he seems mad that Raiden isn't going after the President right away. But call him again, and Campbell discusses whether or not Solid Snake is actually the terrorist leader. Another call wraps up that conversation. Call again and Rose answers this time. She's found some marketing information about the Big Shell. Call her again, and she confirms that an important item may be in Strut F. Another call puts the Colonel back on the line, this time to talk about the nanomachines in Raiden's bloodstream.

Warehouse **Browsing**

Move to the left end of the corridor and collect the **Ration** situated behind the crates. Enter the door that does not have a level marking and find the **M9 Tranquilizer Gun** situated in the space among the stacked boxes. Then collect the two boxes of **M9 Bullets** in the area; Raiden should now have a full supply.

Now that you have the M9, return to Strut A and proceed to Strut B as ordered. With this firearm, you can get the drop on the central guard in Strut A.

DOG TAGS: Strut-A Control Room Guard

Difficulty: Easy

Returning from Strut F with the M9, it's time to collect your first Dog Tags in the Plant chapter. Equip the gun and simply wait until the guard searches the east portion of the room near the FA Connector Bridge entrance. When the guard turns around and walks back to the center, run up and aim your gun at him from behind. Then get in front of him and point the gun at his face to get his Dog Tags.

AB Connecting Bridge

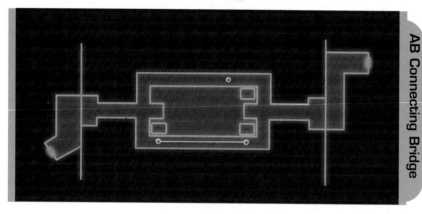

AB Connecting Bridge

Continue on course to Strut B by crossing the AB Connecting Bridge. Raiden notices that two guards are patrolling the platform. The Colonel radios and explains how to avoid the guards by hanging from the rail and shimmying.

AB Bridge **Tactics**

The top guard is stationary and faces the rail; he will easily spot you if you try to cross by shimmying under him. You must cross through the area where the guard is slowly patrolling back and forth. If the guard is at the opposite end, run to the bottom corner. Then face the rail and press ⃤ to jump over and hang. Shimmy across the bridge to the Strut B side. When you jump back onto the platform, aim for the orange-colored section. If Raiden lands on a section of iron grating, the guard will hear.

Dog Tags Can Wait

Avoid attempting to collect Dog Tags at this time. Both of these guards will resist arrest, meaning you must have heavier firepower to convince them.

07713
0328420082 200200151937100214050 19 0151937100

Strut B Transformer Room

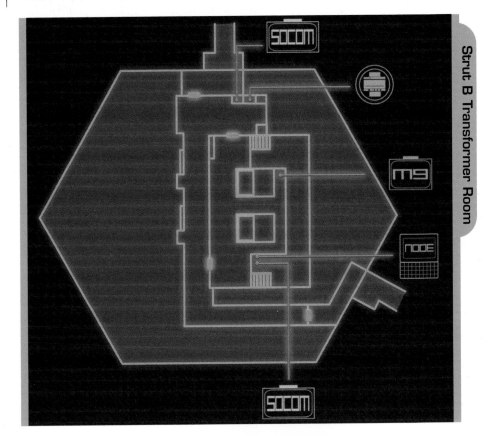

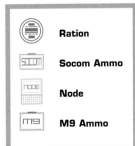

Ration	
Socom Ammo	
Node	
M9 Ammo	

The walls of Strut B are painted in human carnage. Inside the Transformer Room, some sort of vampire-like creature wipes out a group of Navy SEALs. Raiden has just encountered his first Dead Cell member, the supernaturally gifted assassin named Vamp.

After driving off the Romanian scourge, Raiden meets the only surviving member of the squad. He's a shrewd and jaded SEAL 10 operative named Lieutenant Junior Grade Iroquois Pliskin. Pliskin gives Raiden his **Cigarettes** and the unsuppressed **Socom** pistol. Since the gun doesn't have a silencer, stick with the M9 unless you need to destroy an object or a Cypher.

IROQUOIS PLISKIN (David Hayter)

Passing of the Shaver

If you collected the Shaver in the Strut A Deep Sea Dock, the scene where Pliskin gives Raiden some items becomes one sentence longer. Raiden gives the scraggly soldier the Shaver, since he obviously needs it.

Raiden's New Partner

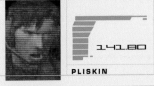

141.80

PLISKIN

Later on, Pliskin will provide expert field advice on weapons and strategy. But for now, the old guy needs a nap. After obtaining Pliskin's frequency during the cinema, tune to the channel and call him repeatedly. Pliskin remains asleep for the time being, but Raiden's reactions are amusing. In the final call, Pliskin screams out in his sleep.

Ongoing Transmission

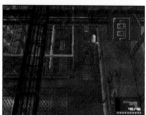

During the meeting between Raiden and Pliskin, the Colonel radios with a message from SEAL 10 team. They're pinned down on the BC connecting bridge, and they need assistance. Raiden has to go alone since Pliskin needs a rest.

Descend the stairs past the dozing Pliskin and grab the **Socom Bullets** sitting next to the Node. Login and download the Strut B map. A box of **M9 Bullets** is on the north side of the upper level. You might be better off leaving these here until you really need them. If you pick up an ammo box just to receive one bullet, you're shortchanging yourself.

There are three lockers near the exit to the BC Connecting Bridge. The right locker holds **Socom Bullets**, and the center has a **Ration**. If you can't pick up one of these items because Raiden's slot is full, leave the locker open so you remember to pick it up later.

BC Connecting Bridge

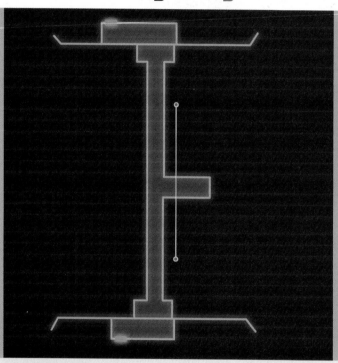

BC Connecting Bridge

Raiden witnesses the final battle between the SEAL Team 10 and the merciless Fortune, the "Queen" of Dead Cell. During the following Codec, the Colonel decides that Dead Cell might retaliate for the SEAL Team's assault by blowing up the Big Shell. Raiden must find a way to locate and defuse the bombs set all around the facility. For advice, he seeks out the wisdom of Navy bomb expert Peter Stillman, who accompanied the SEALs into the Big Shell. Move across the empty bridge, collecting the **Chaff Grenades** dropped by the SEALs. Enter Strut C.

Harrier II and Dead Cell Checks

After the astonishing battle, contact Colonel Campbell repeatedly. He will discuss the specifications on the Harrier II that shot down the cargo helicopters scheduled to pick up the SEALS. Continue pestering him until he and Rose agree to do background checks on the members of Dead Cell.

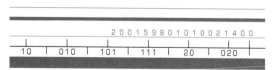

MISSION 02: BOMB DISPOSAL

Colonel Campbell has shifted mission priority to disarming the bombs that have been set all over the plant by the maniacal explosives genius known as Fatman. First, you must find and recruit Navy bomb expert Peter Stillman, who was brought in with the SEAL team. Under his tutelage, it shouldn't be hard to learn what to do and carry out the Colonel's orders.

Strut c Dining Hall

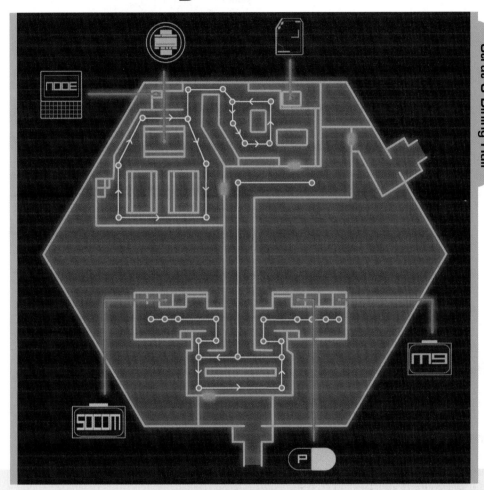

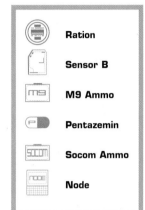

Ration	
Sensor B	
M9 Ammo	
Pentazemin	
Socom Ammo	
Node	

A smart infiltrator will search the bathrooms for useful items—even the Women's! Check the left stall in the Men's Room to find some **Socom Bullets**.

In the Women's Bathroom, check the left toilet stall for **Pentazemin**. The far right stall holds **M9 Bullets**. If you can't carry them right now, leave the door open as a reminder for later.

Start a Background Check

140.85

COLONEL

Call the Colonel twice as you check the bathrooms here, and Raiden will ask about Fortune. Rose offers to dig through some files. She might have some information by the time you reach the next area.

The Bomb Squad Guy

PETER STILLMAN   (Greg Eagles)

Pri...

A poor old man who got dragged along for this picnic.

Continue up the center hallway past a Lv1 door. Raiden meets Peter Stillman, who is going through the kitchen looking for bombs. Stillman explains to Raiden and Pliskin how to clear the C4 bombs from all of the Big Shell's struts. There is a bomb in every strut, and Raiden must clear the ones labeled A through F. Stillman equips Raiden with the **Coolant** and the **Sensor A**. He also gives the rookie the **Lv1 PAN Card**. Start searching for bombs in Strut C.

First Person Viewing Pleasure

Move the Left Analog Stick as Stillman explains how to use the Coolant to defuse a bomb. Raiden can look all around the kitchen, even over at Pliskin.

Bomb Markers

Any time during what we're calling Mission 2, the START screen map will have small markers indicating which buildings have not yet been cleared of bombs.

Explosives Expertise

140.25

STILLMAN

Dial Stillman's frequency on the Codec. He'll give you some pretty obvious clues about where the first bomb is hidden, and he'll even make fun of you for going into the Women's Bathroom.

Bomb Disposal Strategy

141.80

PLISKIN

Now that he's awake, the SEAL officer is a lot more help. After a few calls, he will provide incredibly detailed information, gossip, and character nuances of all the Dead Cell members. He also discusses the dead Navy Captain and his membership in the SEALS, but his answers are rather vague and grouchy.

Beginning the Search

Move into the eating area and download the local map from the Node. Equip Sensor A, and you'll spot a greenish cloud on the map. Fatman's bomb is located somewhere in the cloud, which hovers over the Women's Bathroom.

If you're hungry, there's a **Ration** under the top table in the cafeteria section. Also, you can mess with Stillman's temper by pressing up against the pantry door where he's hidden and knocking. If you try to open the door, he gets even angrier.

Pliskin Moves Fast

141.80

PLISKIN

Immediately after leaving the cafeteria, give Pliskin a ring on the Codec. He has already frozen the first bomb in Shell 2! Raiden already has some catching up to do.

The Strut C Bomb

Enter the Women's Bathroom and stand near the right-hand sink. Look up in First Person View, and you'll immediately spot the bomb. It's tucked into a crevice above the toilet, and it's reflected in the mirror. Equipping the Coolant automatically puts Raiden in Intrusion view. Just aim the Coolant at the bomb and keep spraying it until the device clicks off.

Pliskin the Smart-Alec

141.80

PLISKIN

As you're standing in the Women's Bathroom, call Pliskin for a rather amusing conversation. Call him again, and he talks about the second C4 bomb he just froze. The places he finds the bombs are sometimes funny, and sometimes there are hints about where to search for bombs.

Strut C Tactics

After you meet Stillman and Pliskin in Strut C, leave the level through either exit and then reenter. Guards have taken up posts around the dining area, and it's time to collect some Dog Tags. But don't try these yet unless you have the M9.

STRATEGY

Strut C Corridor Guard

This guard patrols the entire stretch of the corridor on Strut C, as well as the two bathrooms. The easiest location to tranquilize him or take him down is at the bottom end of the corridor, near the bathrooms. Just hide in the Men's Room and watch the radar as he moves down. When he turns to face the Women's Room, run out and nail him.

DOG TAG: Strut C Corridor Guard

Difficulty: Medium

What makes this guard difficult is his timing and patrol route. The cramped and curvy entrances to the restroom are a place where you're likely to foul up a capture. As the guard comes down the central corridor toward the BC Connecting Bridge entrance, stand just inside the Men's Room. As soon as he faces the Women's, run out behind him and get the surprise. Even if he starts moving toward the Women's, you still have time, but once he gets inside the bathroom, abort. There's hardly any room in there to perform the capture correctly, so don't risk getting spotted.

STRATEGY

Strut C Dining Hall Guard

This guard has a long pattern all the way through the kitchen and the cafeteria. The open area is an easy place for him to turn and spot Raiden. If the guard is in the kitchen, stand on the opposite side of the cafeteria and aim a tranquilizer at his head. Don't hit any of the dishes or glasses on the counter in between, because the noise will alert the guard and make him start moving.

DOG TAG: Strut C Dining Hall Guard

Difficulty: Easy

Getting the drop on this guard is somewhat easier than trying to snipe him from a distance. Simply wait outside the south Lv1 door. Once the guard passes the door heading to the bottom corner of the room, run through the door and a few steps toward him. Then capture him by aiming the handgun. Use the dots on the radar to better judge your distance, and wait until he faces west so that you don't have to squeeze between the guard and the wall.

2950010021486 0187

73705011   017

BC Connecting Bridge

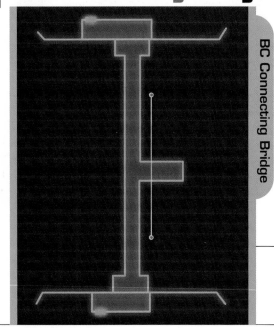

BC Connecting Bridge

A Cypher now patrols the damaged bridge, so be cautious. Use either a Chaff Grenade to get through this area, or use the Socom to knock out the Cypher altogether. To take a Cypher out in one shot, you must hit it directly on the camera.

You must dispose of five more bombs. Due to the enemy placement on the bridges and in the struts, plus the number of quick cutscenes that point out enemy placement, it seems that the easier way to go is counterclockwise through Struts B and A, then F through D.

Strut B

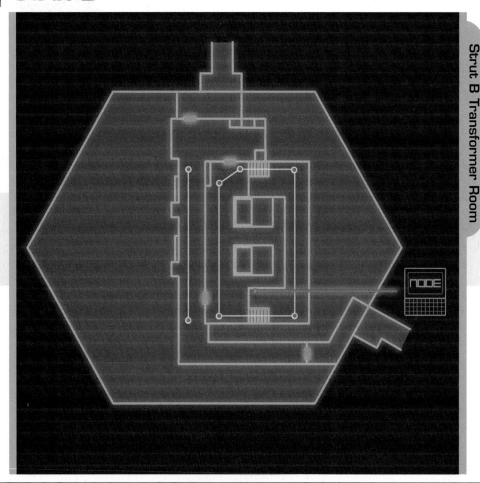

Strut B Transformer Room

NODE	**Node**

Two new guards patrol inside and outside the Transformer Room. Because of their long patrol routes, these guards are pretty easy to take down.

As you move south in the corridor, you might hear a sudden beeping. This is the signal from Fatman's bomb. Inside the north door of the Transformer room, the top transformer's door is open. When you close it, you'll find the second bomb. Use Coolant to freeze it. Then call Stillman for relevant conversation, and check in with Pliskin.

Strut B Tactics

There is a way to get through this area without a guard spotting Raiden. As you're moving from north to south, watch the radar as the guard inside the room moves from north to south on the upper portion. As he begins to descend the stairs on the south side, run through the room. Pause while the guard in the corridor starts walking north, and then exit the south door.

STRATEGY

Strut B Transformer Room Guard

Exercise an extreme amount of caution when dealing with this guard because of the iron floor grates. One of the easiest spots from which to hit this guy is in front of the Node on the lower level. Just stand there until he comes down the south stairs. When he pauses, aim and fire.

STRATEGY

Strut B Corridor Guard

With the M9, Raiden is capable of quieting this guard from the north or south corner. You might find the Dog Tag strategy a little more challenging, however.

DOG TAG: Strut B Transformer Room Guard

Difficulty: Easy

Getting the better of the sentry in the Transformer room isn't too hard. On his route, he pauses by the north door near the lockers and stares for a moment. Simply run through the door and get the drop on him.

DOG TAG: Strut B Corridor Guard

Difficulty: Hard

Due to the high number of floor gratings in the corridor, it is necessary to set up a complex trap for the guard. Cross south through the Transformer Room and enter the corridor through the lower-west door when the guard is moving upward in his route. Open one of the transformer doors in the corridor, press Raiden's back against it, and crouch (⊗) so that Raiden cannot be seen through the door's opening. As the guard passes moving south, stand and press ● to get the drop on him.

AB Connecting Bridge

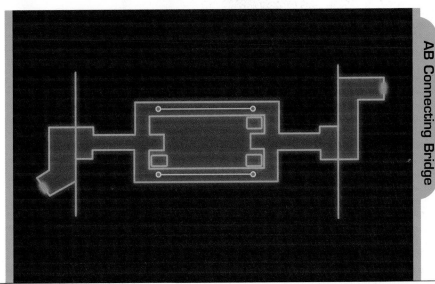

AB Connecting Bridge

Now that Raiden has the Socom, there is a way to get the Dog Tags from at least one of the AB Connecting Bridge Guards. One of the two guards must be tranquilized so that when you fire warning shots at one guard, the other will be asleep and unable to hear. The Dog Tag strategy for both guards here is roughly the same.

AB Bridge Tactics, Part 2

DOG TAG: AB Connecting Bridge Guards (Both)

Difficulty: Very Hard

Approaching from either end, run out onto the bridge just a few feet, so that Raiden stands just outside the guard's cone of vision when he pauses on your side of his route. Enter First Person View and tranquilize the closest guard. Then run to the area behind the guard that is still active, jump over the rail, and hang. Shimmy across the platform a little, so that the guard crosses above as you are shimmying to a position a few feet behind him. When the guard stops at the end of an iron grating, quietly jump onto the platform behind him. Nudge the Left Analog Stick just a little to shake off the jump, and then draw the Socom on the guard. When he taunts, fire a shot into his hand. Then you'll get his tags. Now eliminate the guard and drag him out of view. Move over to the sleeping guard. Equip the Coolant and spray it in the guard's face for a few seconds. When he wakes, run back inside the closest entrance and wait for the guard's cone of vision to change from yellow to white. Now you can employ the same strategy with this guard that you used on the last one. This complex strategy may take a practice run to master, so save your game beforehand.

Strut A Pump Room

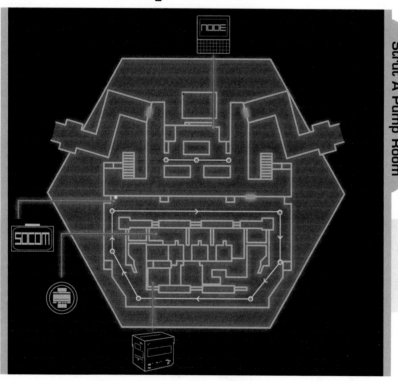

Strut A Pump Room

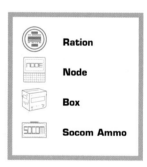

- 🔲 Ration
- 🔳 Node
- 📦 Box
- SOCOM Socom Ammo

With Sensor A equipped, you can tell that Fatman's bomb is hidden somewhere in the mechanical room to the south. Without being seen, move past the guard in the cubicle area or hold him up for his Dog Tags if you haven't already. The Lv1 PAN card will allow Raiden into the machinery room—just be certain that the guard inside is nowhere near the door. Move to the south corner of the room and run over the stairs into the central area of pipes. Crouch and crawl under the pipes, moving upward and then over to the left. A **Ration** is on the far side of this pipe maze.

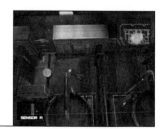

From the Ration, crawl back to the red pipe and crawl south under it until you reach a small square area where the bomb is located. Stay flat on the floor to avoid detection and use the Coolant to deactivate the detonator.

At this point, you may have to take care of the guard; see the following Tactics section. Then move to the bottom-left stairs and crouch on the other side. Crawl to the right under some pipes, then stand and hop over the obstacle to reach **Cardboard Box 1**.

Emerging from the lower part of the pipe maze, and with the guard tranquilized or neutralized, stand on top of the lower-left stairs and aim for the surveillance camera in the top-left corner of the room. Shoot it out, and then claim the **Socom Bullets** that sit under it.

Pump Room Tactics

Be wary of the guard's location before you enter or emerge from the tangle of pipes in the center of the room. This guard really doesn't have to be tranquilized if all you want to do is defuse the bomb and get out of here. The guard cannot see you when you're inside the pipes.

 DOG TAG: Strut A Pump Room Guard

Difficulty: Easy

Hide amongst the pipes on the right side of the room until the guard passes the bottom-right corner. Then follow him to the bottom-left corner where he stops, and aim your weapon to get the drop on him. Be sure to capture him before he walks into the camera's range.

FA Connecting Bridge

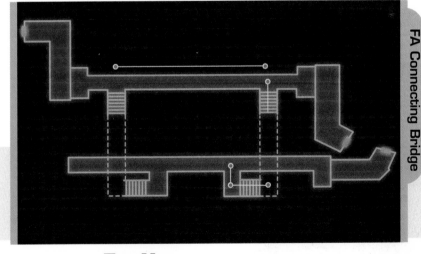

FA Connecting Bridge

A lone soldier has joined the Cypher in patrolling the bridge. To enter Strut F closest to the Node location, use the lower entrance on the Strut F side of the bridge.

FA Bridge Tactics

FA Bridge Cypher and Guard

Wait until the guard is patrolling the lower part of the bridge, and then use the Socom to blow the Cypher out of the sky. With the M9 handy, move out to the halfway point of the bridge. When the guard comes back up to the top, tranquilize him and enter Strut F through the bottom level.

DOG TAG: FA Bridge Guard

Difficulty: Medium

After destroying the Cypher with the Socom, run to the top of the stairs, crouch and hide behind the small corner as shown in the screenshot. When the guard comes up the stairs, stand up and nudge the Left Stick a little, then aim your weapon to capture the guard. There's plenty of room to get in front of him and demand those Dog Tags. This guard will resist capture, so fire a warning shot or blow his hand off.

Strut F **Warehouse**

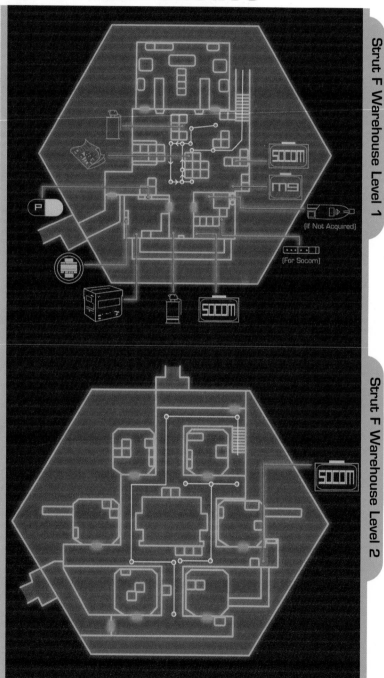

Strut F Warehouse Level 1

Strut F Warehouse Level 2

[If Not Acquired]

[For Socom]

SOCOM	**Socom Ammo**
M9	**M9 Ammo**
	Mine Detector
	Supressor
	Stun Grenades
	Box
	Ration
P	**Pentazemin**
	Book
	Chaff Grenades

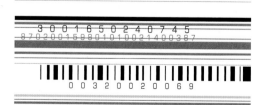

Enter the Warehouse again, this time through the lower B1 level. Immediately press Raiden's back up against the nearby boxes so that the guard does not catch sight of him. When the guard moves north in the room, slip around the crates and into the south passage. A box of **Chaff Grenades** is at the bottom of the passage. Enter the left Lv1 door.

Download the map of the Warehouse from the Node. **Cardboard Box 2** sits in the bottom corner of the room. Of the lockers on the left, the one that is unlocked contains a **Ration**. As for the locked locker, if you stand in the space above it and hit the door repeatedly from the side with single punches, the door will fall outward and you can get the **Book** inside. This naughty magazine will keep any guard distracted for quite some time. In the top row of lockers, the one on the right holds **Pentazemin**.

Use First Person View to locate the vent shaft at floor level. Crawl into the shaft and navigate to the east room. When you emerge, collect the **Socom Suppressor** and **Socom Bullets**. Equip the Socom in the right menu and the Suppressor in the left, and the silencer will be permanently attached to your gun. Climb over the crates and grab the **Mine Detector** on the other side. Some **M9 Bullets** have been stashed under the shelves behind the Mine Detector location.

Now we move on to the business of taking out the guards and collecting the available items in the warehouse. Use the following tactics for maximum efficiency.

Strut F's Bomb

Equip Sensor A, and Fatman's signature appears on the left side of the first floor. The bomb is planted in the middle of a fortress of stacked crates. The only way to reach it is by dropping from the rail above. For success, you'll have to take out all the guards, including the one that reports. Then defuse the bomb quickly and get out of the Warehouse before an investigation commences.

Warehouse Wares

Other items scattered around the warehouse include the **Socom Bullets** on top of a crate. Just get on the crate to get them. **Stun Grenades** are partially hidden among the crates between the two Lv2 doors. You can drop from above to collect **M9 Bullets** in the bottom-right corner of the lower level. You can obtain another **Book**, which is on top of the crates in the center of the room, by dropping from the top-level rail, as well. On the second floor, return to the room where you got the M9 and crawl through the vent. With the Soliton radar, it's much easier to avoid enemy guards as you emerge from the vent. A box of **Socom Bullets** is at the end of the shaft.

To Each According to Need

Take only what you need from the Warehouse when you really need it, because you will have to return to Strut F several more times before the day is done.

Warehouse Tactics

Three guards patrol the Warehouse, making it one of the most difficult places to get through. One guard patrols above, one guard patrols below, and the guard who reports in every few minutes moves from the upper level to the lower level at will. Every move you make in this place needs to be carefully calculated, starting with the moment you enter. You'll have to collect Dog Tags as you go because Raiden's movements here are so restricted.

Warehouse B1 Guard

Make this guard your first target. Enter the Warehouse through the B1 level entrance from the FA Connecting Bridge. Sneak around this guard and download the map from the Node. After you collect the Mine Detector from the lower-right Lv1 room on B1, wait until the guard pauses for a long moment directly outside the door. Also, make sure that another guard is not patrolling the lower floor. Step out and take care of the guard, then drag his body into the southwest room and stuff him in a locker for safe keeping

DOG TAG: Warehouse B1 Guard

Difficulty: Easy

When using the strategy described to the left, run out of the southeast room and capture the guard from behind. Try to catch him as close to the south end as possible so that the guards above cannot see what you are doing. After you have threatened him, tranquilize him and drag him into a locker inside the southwest Lv1 room. *Do not execute him*, or the blood will attract the wrong kind of attention.

Warehouse 1F Guard

After tranquilizing the guard who only patrols B1, exit the Warehouse through the B1 door, out to the FA Connecting Bridge. Move to the top entrance and come back into the Warehouse. The guard who only patrols the upper level moves in a U-shaped pattern around the east side of the rail. Return to the room where Raiden obtained the M9 and crawl into the duct.

This duct emerges in a small alcove to the left of the main area. This guard occasionally checks the alcove, so make sure that you aren't seen emerging from the vent. Hide behind the low crates. Once the other guard moves down to the B1 level, prepare to move on the 1F guard. As the guard moves north along his route, catch him by surprise from behind. *Do not execute him—just tranquilize him!* The blood will draw unwanted suspicion at this critical juncture. If you can, quickly drag the body into the alcove where the vent exits so that the remaining guard doesn't spot it.

DOG TAG: Warehouse 1F Guard

Difficulty: Hard

The hard part is waiting for the other guard to go away so you can have a moment alone with this one. Follow the strategy outlined above. When the guard moves north in his patrol route, run out from your hiding space and surprise him from behind. Move in front of him and quickly demand those Dog Tags. This guard should cave easily.

Warehouse Reporting Guard

You should take care of the other two guards before you go after this one. Once you've taken care of the upper level guard, wait on the upper level for this one to come back upstairs. His patrol route takes him down the west side of the room, then down into the south corridor near the FA Connecting Bridge entrance. When he moves to that point, move to the top of the south corridor and take him out.

DOG TAG: Warehouse Reporting Guard

Difficulty: Medium

Follow the strategy outlined above as closely as possible, but get really close behind him in the south corridor. Even after all your hard work, this surly mutt has the audacity to scoff at Raiden's threats. Now that the Socom is silenced, you can't scare guards by firing loud warning shots anymore. You have to shoot this guard in the hand to show him you mean business. Once you have those tags, quickly dispose of this guard and get to work on diffusing the bomb in the area.

EF Connecting Bridge

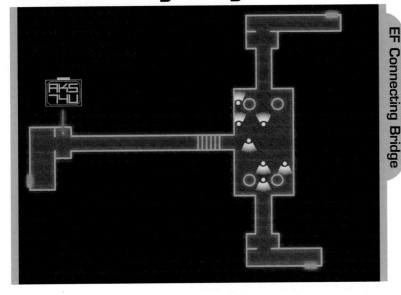

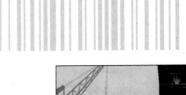

	**AKS-74u Ammo**

Raiden watches as a guard ascends to a high lookout point on the Heliport. From there, the sentry uses binoculars to search the bridge for intruders. Where is a long-range sniper rifle when you need one? Carefully aim the M9 at the guard and put him out of commission in order to cross.

Moving onto the platform, a mysterious person calling himself "Mr. X" contacts Raiden and warns him that Claymore mines are set on the bridge. Raiden will store Mr. X's frequency, but the enigmatic figure cannot be contacted for help at any time. There are two ways to detect Claymores, either with the Thermal Goggles or a Mine Detector. Crawling across a Claymore allows Raiden to pick it up. So in that sense, there are **7 Claymores** to collect on the bridge.

Strut E Parcel Room, 1F

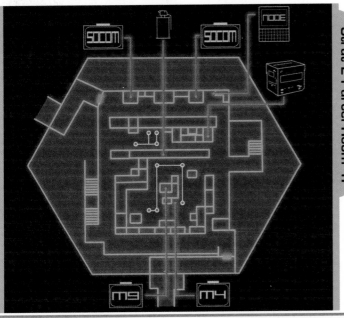

Node	**Node**
Box	**Box**
	Stun Grenades
SOCOM	**Socom Ammo**
M9	**M9 Ammo**
M4	**M4 Ammo**

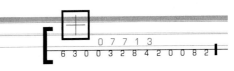

When entering the Parcel Room from the north end, the guard posted nearby will immediately spot Raiden. Entering from the EF Connecting Bridge is much easier. Wait in the south alcove and peek around the corner. Look for the guard with the U-shaped patrol route in the south area to come into view. When that guard turns and heads north, it's time to move. Navigate carefully through the west side of the area, using the large conveyors as cover. Move to the top-right corner of the room, where the Node is located. Download the map of Strut E. There are several items to pick up here, but the guards also have extremely good visibility despite all the fast-moving boxes. Use the following strategies to take them down so you can collect the items.

Cardboard Box 5, which is the *Zone of the Enders* box, is on top of the conveyor to the northeast. This is not a good box to hide in because it is so awesome that it will attract some guards rather than provide concealment. To get **Stun Grenades**, crawl under the conveyor behind the guard that makes periodic reports. Naturally, both guards should be heavily slumbering before you try for either of these items.

At the south end of a bunch of Tokugawa boxes in the lower center of the room, there are **M4 Bullets** that you can collect later on. Crawl under two of the shelves at the top end of the room for two boxes of **Socom Bullets**. If Raiden is desperate for **Rations**, there are some in a small vent at the bottom of the western stairs.

Rations are in a vent at Raiden's feet.

Parcel Room Tactics

After you reach the Node at the top of the room and login, the two guards here become relatively easy to take down. Collecting their Dog Tags is another matter.

Parcel Room Patrolling Guard

After you avoid the guard's line of sight during his first patrol, move to the bottom of the stairs in the small alcove on the east side of the room. From here, enter First Person View and wait for the guard to come into sight and stop. Quickly target him with the M9 and raise your sighting up to his head. If the reporting guard is staring south when you happen to pull the trigger, even better. He will come around to see why the other guard has fallen, and he lines up directly in your sights, too.

DOG TAG: Parcel Room Patrolling Guard

Difficulty: Hard

To obtain this guard's tags, you essentially have to rush him. Move to the second large machine from the top on the east side of the room, near the stairs entrance. When the guard reaches the eastern end of his route, run down and catch him. Adding to the difficulty is the fact that as you run south, machinery and other tall pieces obstruct your view. Use the radar to determine if you are close enough to the guard to draw. This strategy can be intimidating, but it seems to work every time.

Parcel Room Reporting Guard

Killing or tranquilizing a guard who has to report every few minutes is not wise, because others outside the area will become suspicious. Avoid messing with this guard if you can. This guard can barely see anything the way he's pigeonholed himself into this tiny space. Getting past him isn't that difficult. The items that surround this guard are not that essential to your mission, so you can determine the best course of action.

DOG TAG: Parcel Room Reporting Guard

Difficulty: Hard

To get the drop on this guard, you must first take out or tranquilize the other guard. Rushing up to this guard is no problem because he stares north for the longest time. From the east side of the room, watch this sentry carefully. Wait for him to examine the south side of the room, and then turn back. This is when to run up behind him. But wait; it is even better to stand right there and allow the guard to radio in his next report. Then aim your weapon to capture him. When you get in front of the guard, he will refuse to cooperate. You must shoot the guard in the hand or the shoulder to get your point across.

Strut E **Heliport**

Strut E Heliport

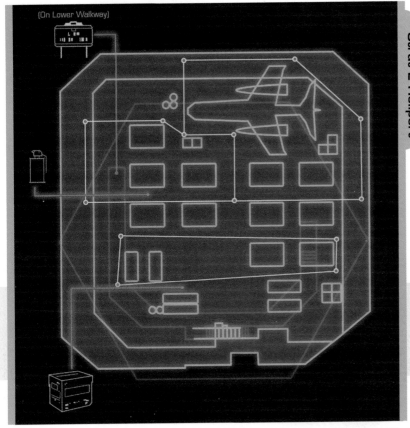

(On Lower Walkway)

	Box
	Stun Grenades
	Claymore Mines

Moving to the base of the stairs, up to the helicopter landing pad, Raiden overhears a radio conversation that a Russian woman named Olga is having. Making a familiar mistake, Raiden attempts to arrest the woman, but fails.

After the cut-scene, go back down the stairs and cross to the left side. Someone has knocked out the guard that is posted here! Shake down the guard's body to get an item, and grab the **Claymores** on the other side of him.

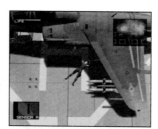

Return to the stairs and ascend to the heliport. From the top of the stairs, move to the left and collect **Cardboard Box 3**. **Stun Grenades** are between two freight cars on the west side of the building.

The terrorist's Harrier fighter jet is parked here, and two guards make wide sweeps of the area. Using Sensor A, you can see that Fatman's scent is all over the Harrier. Move to just under the wing of the fighter, crouch, and use First Person View. The bomb is stuffed way up under the jet, directly under its landing gear. Position Raiden under the Harrier's wing and use the Coolant on the bomb. Due to the extreme range, this bomb will take longer to defuse than the others.

Heliport Tactics

The guards on the Heliport patrol areas so far from each other that it's quite easy to stalk each of them individually to take them out. For this reason, we need only tell you how to obtain their Dog Tags. Be certain that both guards are snoring when you defuse the bomb under the Harrier.

DOG TAG: South Heliport Guard

Difficulty: Easy

The guard who patrols the portion of the Heliport closest to the stairway entrance makes a long cross from east to west. At some point on this route, you can position Raiden behind one of the freight transports where the guard will pass. As the guard keeps moving, run out from your hiding place and chase down the fast-moving guard.

DOG TAG: North Heliport Guard

Difficulty: Medium

This guard patrols around the Harrier jet, which makes his route a little difficult to follow. But there is a point directly between the Harrier and the freight containers where the guard stops and stands facing north for a long moment. This is the best time to run out from behind a container and surprise the guard from behind.

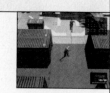

DOG TAGS: Lower Walkway Guard

Difficulty: Medium

After you've diffused the bomb under the Harrier, the guard who looks out over the DE Connecting Bridge is alert and actively patrols a long route. He will move down the walkway almost to the stairs, so stay put just out of sight range. When the guard turns and heads back to his lookout point, run steadily behind him until Raiden finally catches up. Then hold up the guard and get those tags. Tranquilizing this guard before moving on also makes it easier to cross the DE Connecting Bridge!

DE Connecting Bridge

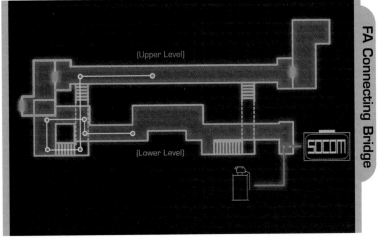

(Upper Level)

(Lower Level)

FA Connecting Bridge

SOCOM

Stun Grenades

SOCOM Socom Ammo

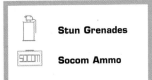

If the lookout on the Heliport above has been recently put to sleep or dispatched, then crossing this narrow path is much less treacherous. Descend the first set of stairs on the left and move back to the ending to collect **Socom Bullets** and **Stun Grenades**.

DE Bridge Tactics

Since there is only one guard aside from the one overhead, you could easily tranquilize the guard and run directly across the bridge easy as pie. However, there is a reward to be gained from exerting a little more effort.

DOG TAG: DE Bridge Guard
Difficulty: Easy (once you read this strategy)
Watch for the guard to descend to the lower level, and then run across the top of the bridge. Stop just outside the entrance to Strut D, turn, and watch the guard come back upstairs. He never turns to look toward Strut D! As he moves toward Strut E, follow him to the end of his patrol route and catch him off guard.

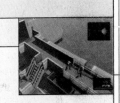

Strut D Sediment Pool

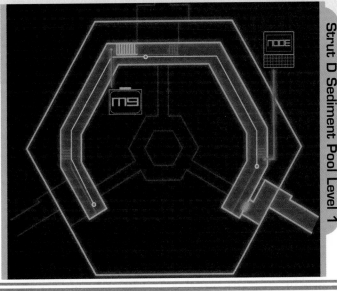

Strut D Sediment Pool Level 1

NODE

m9

M9 M9 Ammo

NODE Node

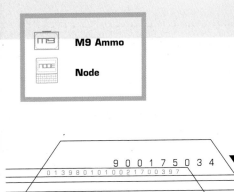

9 0 0 1 7 5 0 3 4   0 8 4
0 1 3 9 8 0 1 0 1 0 0 2 1 7 0 0 3 9 7

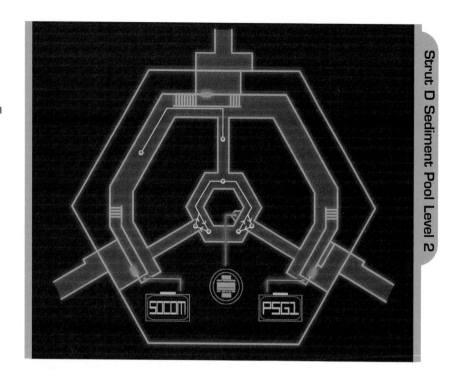

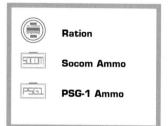

- Ration
- **SOCOM** Socom Ammo
- **PSG1** PSG-1 Ammo

97 001236

Enter Strut D through the lower entrance from the DE Connecting Bridge. The local network Node sits just inside the doorway. Download the essential Soliton Radar map of the area and exit the way you came in. Now reenter the Sediment Pool through the Lv1 entrance.

A box of **PSG-1 Bullets** is just below the upper level entrance. These will have to wait until you have the proper weapon. But from this location, you can safely study the patrol routes and movement patterns of the three guards. The one on the lower level has the longest route, and he must report in every 20 seconds or so. He should be the last one you attack. Start with the soldier in the center, and then do the one near the descending stairs. A **Ration** is in the center of the area, and **Socom Bullets** are near the CD Connecting Bridge exit. A box of **M9 Bullets** is behind the stairs under the Shell 1-2 Bridge exit.

The bomb is located on the lower level under the CD Bridge exit. There are hatches in the floor you can open. Although Fatman's signature odor covers the entire southwestern section, the bomb is located under the last hatch. It's not hard to completely avoid the bottom guard and get over to the bomb before he completes his route. If it comes to it, a little beauty sleep never hurt anyone, either.

Taking Out the Trash

There is a gate that can swing out for waste disposal below the Lv3 door that leads out to the Shell 1-2 Connecting Bridge. This is a good location to drag the bodies of unconscious guards. Just don't dispose of any when the reporting guard is directly below.

Why are you late with your status report?

Circus Acrobatics

One way to reach the bottom level from the top is somewhat daredevil and crazy. Leap over the rail and hang. Then press ⊗ to drop. While Raiden descends, quickly press △ to grab onto the rail below. If you time it right, it's like an express elevator between levels. If not, Raiden drowns in toxic waste.

When All the Bombs Are Frosty...

With the last bomb defused, Raiden reports to Stillman. The bomb expert suspects that an undetectable bomb is at the bottom of Strut A. He has made a new bomb sensor, which is capable of finding odorless bombs by sonar sound waves. Raiden must now return to Strut C and collect Stillman's new sensor.

Sediment Pool Tactics

To cross the top area, Raiden only needs to stand just inside the entrance and target the two guards on the top level. Once they are properly at rest, attend to the matters of the bomb and steer clear of the remaining soldier. Try to leave the reporting guard alone so that a second team is not dispatched to the area. Collecting Dog Tags will require some scary maneuvers.

DOG TAG: Sediment Pool Central Guard

Difficulty: Medium

Go after the center guard first and spread out from there. From just inside the DE Bridge exit, use First Person View to study the center guard's movement pattern and especially his timing. When he is on the opposite side of the center cage from Raiden's position, move to the level just below the entrance, where the PSG-1 Bullets sit. When the guard faces southwest, it's time to move. Run up to the center cage and press Raiden's back into the small niche where the Ration sits. As the center guard moves north, run out and catch him. You can't let him get too far, or the other guard might spot the two of you. Once you have the guard's tags, tranquilize him and drag the body behind the center cage, out of view of the next guard.

DOG TAG: Sediment Pool North Guard

Difficulty: Hard

First, take down the central guard and position Raiden behind the cage opposite the north guard's southernmost stopping point. At this position, the guard will face south for a long time. Then he will search left and right a few times. Move out from behind the cage and stand a few feet closer in. Finally, he turns and faces the Shell 1-2 Connecting Bridge exit for a long moment. This is when you should run up behind him and try to surprise the guard. Best of luck.

DOG TAG: Sediment Pool Lower Level Reporting Guard

Difficulty: Very Hard

Because the lower guard makes such long trips back and forth on the bottom level, he has a great ability to spot Raiden from yards away. The trick to getting the drop on this soldier involves literally getting the drop. Move Raiden to one side of the upper level or the other, wherever the reporting guard is currently patrolling. Wait for the guard to reach the end of his route. Watch on the radar as the sentry turns and moves back in the other direction. At this instant, jump over the rail and hang. Press ✕ to drop, and then quickly press △ to catch the lower level's rail. Hop onto the platform and run up behind the reporting guard. Once you have this guard's tags, high tail it out of Strut D before someone starts demanding a status report.

CD Connecting Bridge

CD Connecting Bridge

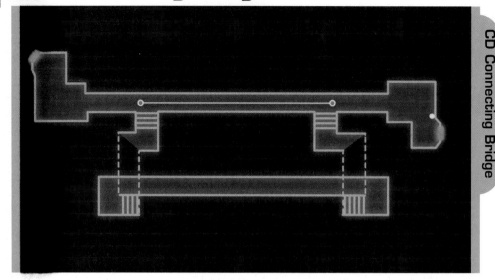

Stepping out of the smelly disposal area, Raiden spots a surveillance camera mounted directly overhead! Swiftly equip the suppressed Socom and use First Person View to shoot the camera.

A lone guard patrols the entire length of the bridge. Wait until he checks the Strut D side, and then turns to go back. Run out and try to get the drop on him!

Booby Trapped Bridge

Use extreme caution crossing the lower bridge; its floor panels are rigged to drop out from under you as you step on them. There are a few methods to cross safely. You can hang and shimmy by hand from outside the rail. If you move quickly, you can run across, but you can do this only once—the panels that drop will be gone the next time you want to cross. Probably the easiest way is to press your body against the rail and sidestep along the length of the bridge.

Strut C Dining Hall

Return to the Kitchen area and find **Sensor B** in the pantry. When Pliskin defuses the last C4 bomb in the Shell 2 strut, the *real* bombs begin counting down. Now you must return to the bottom of Strut A and find the hidden bomb using the new Sensor B. You'll see a countdown of 400 seconds begin ticking away on the right side of the screen. If you don't make it in time, everyone dies!

1024013295001002

Strut A Roof

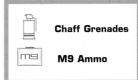

Chaff Grenades

M9 Ammo

14860187

The elevator to the docks has returned to the roof. The guard at the south end won't be much of a nuisance if you get on the elevator quickly. However, the guard does have a set of Dog Tags, and he disappears for a while after the coming events. Better to get the drop on him now if you've got a few seconds to spare. Move to the back of the elevator and it will begin to descend.

Strut A Roof Tactics

Putting down the lone guard is easy. Just move to the southwest corner of the roof and aim at the guard in First Person View as he's crossing the south part of the area away from you. Getting his Dog Tags isn't much harder.

DOG TAG: Strut A Roof Guard
Difficulty: Very Easy
To capture the guard on the roof, enter from either side and carefully follow him around the roof, hiding behind crates when necessary. When the guard stops at the center point in front of the elevator, it's a great time to run out and capture him.

Limited Communication

1Ч0.85

COLONEL

Following the massive explosion in Shell 2, all sources of outside information are severed. The only field support for Raiden now is Colonel Campbell, and Rose at his frequency. Campbell helps Raiden get a grip on his tumultuous emotions and discusses the intentions of the terrorists.

Strut A Deep Sea Dock

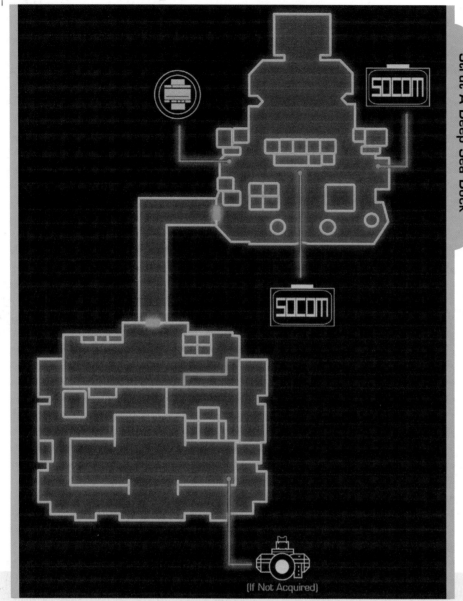

(If Not Acquired)

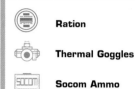

	Ration
	Thermal Goggles
	Socom Ammo

024013295001002148601 87

97001236

Notice that the crates at the dock have all been rearranged. New items are available, too, including a **Ration** and two boxes of **Socom Bullets**. Move through the dock and the short corridor back to Raiden's entry point.

The bomb is located on the underside of the suspended deep sea sub. To defuse it, stand just south of the sub on the side of the pool behind the rail, and use the Coolant from a distance. Move back toward the elevator.

BOSS FIGHT

Fortune

Gender:	Female
Affiliation:	Dead Cell Leader
Weapon:	Lockheed RG-590 Experimental Aircraft Rail Cannon

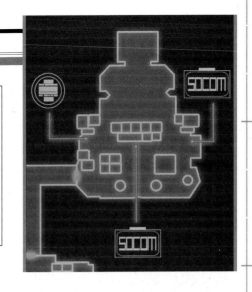

When Raiden nears the elevator, Fortune emerges. She begins to blast every object in the area with her large rail cannon. What's worse is that Fortune can't be hit by Raiden's attacks. Avoid taking a direct hit, because the damage is massive.

Hurry, kill me please!

Don't waste any ammo in this exhibition match, just dodge her attacks and stay away from fires that break out. Keep moving, rolling from one side of the room to the other. If you allow Fortune to pound away at one hiding spot, then soon you won't have anyplace left to hide.

Suddenly the battle ends and the Colonel calls. Fatman has planted a new bomb on the Strut E Heliport and has asked for Raiden to join him there now.

"Lady Luck," also known as "Fortune." Her real name is Helena Dolph Jackson, the daughter of Marine Commander Scott Dolph who was killed aboard the U.S.S. Discovery two years ago, and widow of Colonel Reginald Jackson, former head of the Navy's anti-terrorist training unit, Dead Cell. Fortune joined the military following her father's death. She was singled out and promoted for her one unique talent: her miraculous luck. Fortune was assigned to Dead Cell, where she met her husband. But while luck seems to have blessed her with a superhuman ability, destiny cursed her yet again when her husband was court-martialed on charges of corruption and misappropriation of funds. Since then, Fortune has marshaled leadership of Dead Cell, and the group is now responsible for a myriad of true terrorist attacks on the civilian population.

FORTUNE

FORTUNE (Maula Gale)

My name is Fortune, lucky in war and nothing else..

Strut A Roof

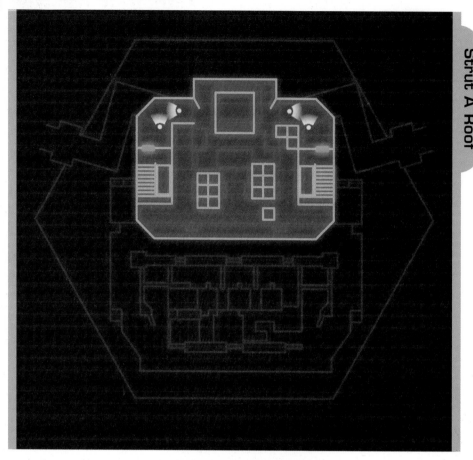

Raiden has 400 seconds to get back to Strut E. The trip is not far if you go through Strut F. On the roof, equip the Mine Detector in order to see the new Claymores that have been set in front of each doorway.

Outside the Pump Room, the guards' patrol patterns have changed. It is easier if you use the east stairs to descend.

Strut E Heliport

Restock your **Socom Bullets** at the top of the stairs because you will desperately need them in a few moments. The bomb you seek is placed conspicuously in the middle of the floor. Defuse it with the Coolant, and Fatman appears.

9 0 0 1 7 5 0 3 4   0 8 4 1 5

0 1 3 9 8 0 1 0 1 0 0 2 1 7 0 0 3 9 7

1 1 3 7 0   0 2 0 0 6

BOSS FIGHT

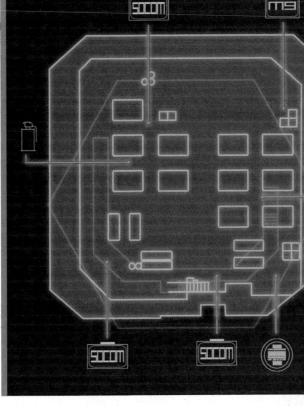

Fatman

Gender:	Male
Affiliation:	Dead Cell Explosives Expert
Weapon:	Semtex C4 Packs with Timed Detonators, UZI 9mm

During this tricky battle, Raiden must defuse bombs as he avoids Fatman's gunfire, and he has to figure out a way to kill the giant man, as well. Keep Sensor A equipped at all times, and use a Ration manually when necessary. Fatman will set two or three bombs around the Heliport. Then he will watch Raiden try to find and defuse them all.

If Raiden is at the right place at the right time, shooting Fatman with the Socom can prevent him from setting a bomb.

In the last half of the battle, Fatman will hang around one of the locations where he set a bomb and will try to defend it. First, knock Fatman down with Socom fire or punches and kicks, and then put a bullet in his head as he tries to recover. He should skate away, allowing you to freely defuse the bomb.

As Fatman tries to set more bombs, chase him down and fire at him with the Socom. Or, if Fatman stops in close range of Raiden, try to knock Fatman down with punches and kicks. Either way, once Fatman is down, equip the Socom and enter First Person View. When Fatman struggles to his hands and knees, shoot him in the head to inflict damage. If he charges at Raiden, flip-jump out of the way. The same goes for when he fires a volley of shots at Raiden.

If Fatman's life gauge is extremely low, take a chance on skipping the bomb disposal and go after Fatman. The battle ends when Fatman's life bar is empty, and any bombs that are ticking away at that time will be cancelled.

When the battle ends, Fatman sets one last bomb. The secret is that it's under Fatman, so drag away his bloated carcass to reveal it. Fatman should drop **Peter Stillman's Dog Tags**. Defuse the final bomb.

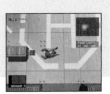

11010
071230154801010034320019

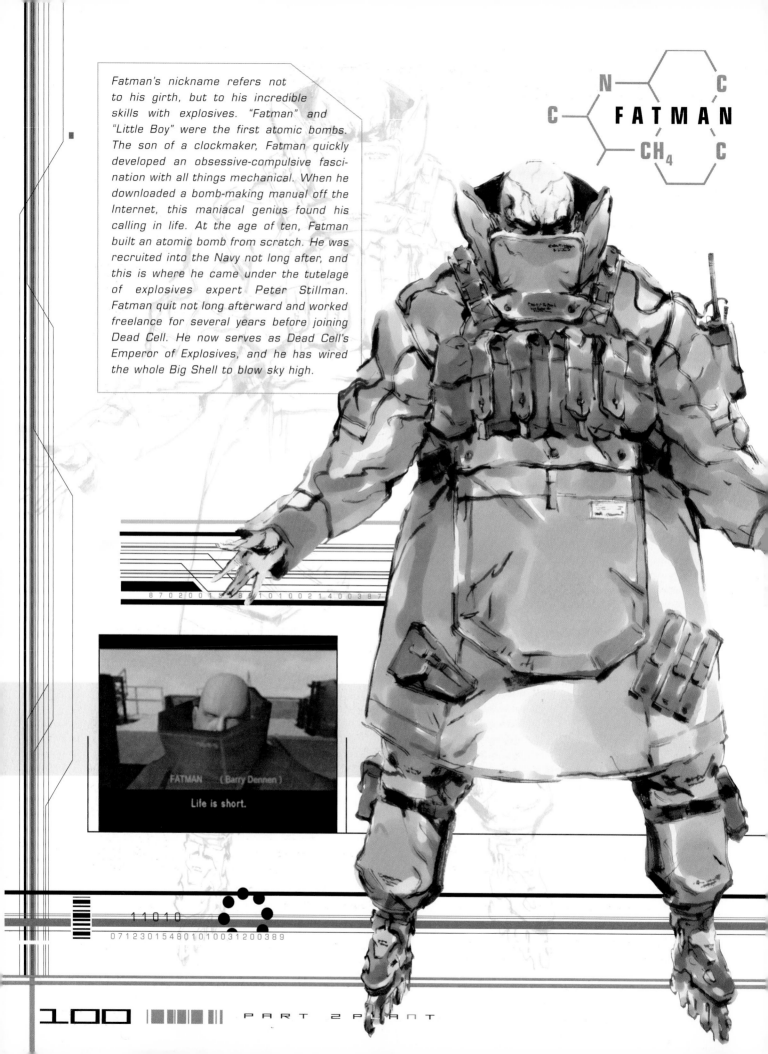

Fatman's nickname refers not to his girth, but to his incredible skills with explosives. "Fatman" and "Little Boy" were the first atomic bombs. The son of a clockmaker, Fatman quickly developed an obsessive-compulsive fascination with all things mechanical. When he downloaded a bomb-making manual off the Internet, this maniacal genius found his calling in life. At the age of ten, Fatman built an atomic bomb from scratch. He was recruited into the Navy not long after, and this is where he came under the tutelage of explosives expert Peter Stillman. Fatman quit not long afterward and worked freelance for several years before joining Dead Cell. He now serves as Dead Cell's Emperor of Explosives, and he has wired the whole Big Shell to blow sky high.

FATMAN

FATMAN   (Barry Dennen)

Life is short.

MISSION 03: HOSTAGE SITUATION

Fatman is dead and the bomb crisis has been averted. But the power still lies in the hands of the terrorists, and Raiden learns this through an unlikely meeting.

Strut E Heliport

I'm like you...I have no name.

Raiden receives a call from the Colonel after defeating Fatman. It's time to go to Shell 1, so you'll want to return to the EF Bridge. Moving back to the stairs, Raiden encounters a Cyborg Ninja wearing an exoskeleton.

The Ninja spells out how to find the President—by going to Shell 1 and finding a hostage named Ames. You'll have to disguise yourself in the **B.D.U.** (body disguise uniform) that the Ninja hands you. Also, you'll have to acquire an AKS-47u. The Ninja gives Raiden a **Cell Phone** so that he can contact Raiden again. When the Ninja calls, the phone buzzes and the controller vibrates. The phone will display an email message. Now you just have to go find the appropriate gun, and the new **Lv2 PAN card** that the Ninja gives you will help. Return to the Strut F warehouse after detouring briefly to engage some new guards.

This security card will unlock all level 2 security doors.

Words of the Ninja

141.80

PLISKIN

Contacting Pliskin a few times, Raiden will ask about the Ninja and the hostage named Ames. Unfortunately, Pliskin is starting to become rather tight-lipped about the events and won't share much background information. What is he afraid of revealing?

Spankin' New Guards

Following Fatman's grand finale, there are new guards posted on three bridges. So, instead of heading back to the Shell 1 entrance by the quick route, we'll show you how to bag the Dog Tags from the three new guards.

DOG TAG: New DE Connecting Bridge Guard

Difficulty: Medium

The guard you've already taken the tags from is patrolling the top level of the bridge, so aim from a distance to put him to sleep. The new guard patrols the lower area, and he can see well in all directions. Entering from the Strut E side, sneak down the stairs to the first corner and wait for the guard to walk toward Strut E. The sentry then turns and walks past the stairs. Sneak down the stairs and catch the guard as he is moving toward Strut D, then squeeze in front of him to demand the tags. Your gun may be sticking through his face, but he will still cower and beg for mercy.

DOG TAG: New CD Connecting Bridge Guard

Difficulty: Medium

Entering from Strut D, the guard you've already taken down is patrolling closer to Strut C. Take the old guard out of the equation with a tranquilizer. Move onto the bridge and hide behind one of the low walls on either side of the entrance. When the new guard climbs the stairs, he patrols toward Strut C first. Allow him to patrol toward Strut D. Then, as he's going back to the stairs, run out and get the drop on him.

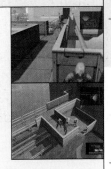

DOG TAG: New BC Connecting Bridge Guard

Difficulty: Medium

First, hide inside the shelter of the Strut C entrance and use the suppressed Socom to blow the Cypher out of the sky. Then watch the guard carefully. After he patrols the short section of destroyed bridge, he comes toward Strut C. Hide until he turns and heads back for Strut B, then run onto the bridge and catch up with him.

EF Connecting Bridge

Don't Rely on the Disguise Yet

Although Raiden can now disguise himself as a Russian mercenary, his uniform indicates that he is supposed to be stationed inside Shell 1. So, the disguise is not useful in other areas of the Big Shell. Use the same sneaking methods as before to return to the EF Connecting Bridge.

This bridge connects not only the two Struts, but is also the east entrance to Shell 1. However, Raiden still needs to find an AKS-74u like the guards use, or his disguise will be incomplete. The Lv2 PAN card allows Raiden to enter doors inside the Warehouse that he couldn't previously, so go look for new items there.

Another Mechanical Foe

Note that a Gun-mounted Cypher enters the area as Raiden reaches Strut F. This formidable surveillance attack equipment will be waiting when you come back...

Strut F Warehouse

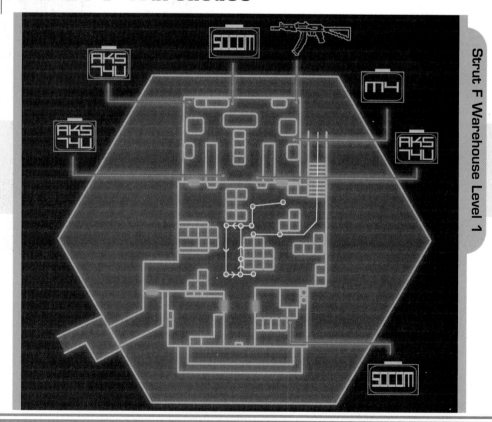

Strut F Warehouse Level 1

	AKS-74u
	AKS-74u Ammo
	Socom Ammo
	M4 Ammo

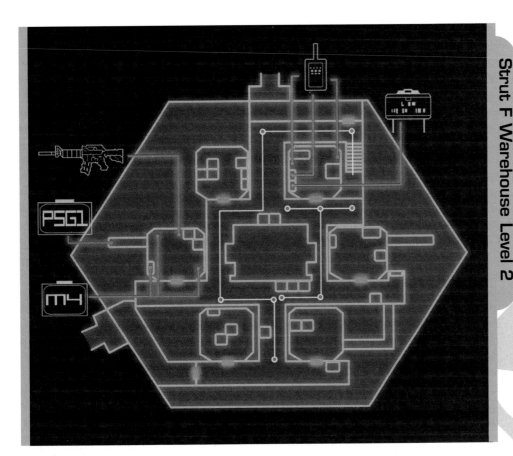

AKS-74u	
Claymore Mine	
C-4	
PSG1	PSG-1 Ammo
M4	M4 Ammo

The AKS-74u isn't the only new item you can obtain in the warehouse. Take down all the guards as efficiently as possible, search the area quickly, and get out before another team is dispatched to investigate. The following Tactics section describes a way to take down all three guards with relative ease.

The northern Lv2 room on the upper level has two lockers where you can conveniently stuff sleeping guards. There are **Claymores** in the lower locker, and there is **C4** in the upper locker. Two more boxes of **C4** lie on the floor in the room.

Carefully navigate to the west side of the upper level, and enter the Lv2 room here. *Do not move too far into the room*—there is an IR beam array wired to Semtex explosives scattered around the room. The control box sits on top of the lockers, so use the suppressed Socom to take it out. The **M4 Assault Rifle** is on the other side of the beams. A box of **M4 ammo** lies nearby, and another one is in the locker. Some **PSG-1 Bullets** are in the small crawlway on the west side of the room. Remember their location for when you actually find a sniper rifle.

To reach the lower level, we recommend exiting out to the FA Connecting Bridge and then reentering through the bottom door. Sneak into the north room with the two Lv2 doors. The **AKS-74u** is in the northeast corner of the room. Three boxes of **AKS-74u Bullets** are scattered around the room, there are **Socom Bullets** to the north, and **M4 Bullets** on the east wall. While you are downstairs, there is a new box of **Socom Bullets** in the southeast Lv1 room. Spend the time to obtain them only if you are very low on ammo.

Strut F Tactics

The Dog Tag strategies for these three guards have already been described, and you already have a good idea of how to take down these guards. We'll just provide some good tips for getting around the Warehouse undiscovered.

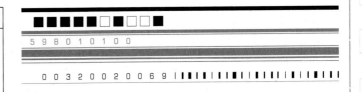

5 9 8 0 1 0 1 0 0

0 0 3 2 0 0 2 0 0 6 9

When you first enter Strut F through the north door on the upper level, the guard who stays on the second floor should be patrolling at the south end of the entrance corridor. While in First Person View, carefully peek out around the corner using R2, and knock this guard out with a single tranquilizer dart. If you miss, he will step into the corridor and probably detect your presence. Drag his body into the upper-right Lv2 room. Stuff him in one of the lockers for safe keeping.

As you navigate the upper level, avoid the guard who reports in, and exit to the FA Connecting Bridge. Reenter Strut F on the bottom floor, where the guard should be facing east for a long moment. Tranquilize him from a distance, then drag his body into the lower-left Lv1 room and stuff him in a locker. Now you can get all the items in the Lv2 security room without much hassle.

Despondent Colonel

140.85

COLONEL

The colonel explains how the disguise works, and that Raiden needs to find the AKS-74u in order to complete the illusion. He also explicitly warns Raiden not to trust Pliskin, which seems a little strange considering the circumstances. In further conversations, Rose promises to look up information on Ames. This could prove very helpful in finding him.

EF Connecting Bridge

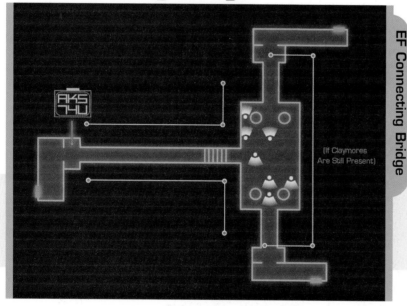

EF Connecting Bridge

(If Claymores Are Still Present)

AKS-74u Ammo

300010

9 7 0 0 1 2 3 6

0 2 0 0 1 2 5 5

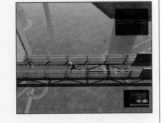

A guard will climb the stairs and act as a lookout over the bridge. Raiden must carefully tranquilize him before moving on. While you are taking care of that, a Gun Cypher will move into view. Use the Socom and aim for its camera. If you're out of Socom Bullets, the M4 Assault Rifle works even better. Run onto the bridge and use First Person View to find the Gun Cypher that now appears over near Shell 1. Shoot out this robot sentry, and then move to the top of the stairs on the left side. Use First Person View to locate another new Gun Cypher that will make life difficult if you try to cross the bridge.

Remember the Rigged Bridge

In a moment, you'll see why it's important to take out all the Gun Cyphers. As Raiden crosses the bridge, the floor panels will fall out of it. If Raiden just keeps running, he should get across safely. But if a Gun Cypher hits him and he is stopped for even a second, he'll fall to his death.

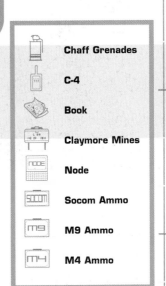

AKS-74u Bullets are on the bridge outside Shell 1. Outside the Shell 1 door, equip the AKS-74u and the B.D.U. Raiden is now disguised and ready to infiltrate.

Shell 1 Core, 1F

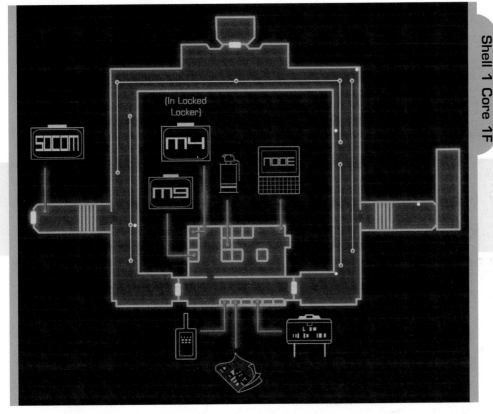

Shell 1 Core 1F

(In Locked Locker)

Chaff Grenades	
C-4	
Book	
Claymore Mines	
Node	
Socom Ammo	
M9 Ammo	
M4 Ammo	

Maintaining Your Cover

With both the B.D.U. and the AKS-74u equipped, be careful not to bump into any of the guards, or your cover will be blown! If you do bump into a guard, knock him out with kicks and punches and put your disguise back on before any other guards spot you. If you can move some distance away and disguise yourself again before the guard gets back up, not even the guard that previously spotted you will be able to identify you again.

Also, do not crouch and crawl in front of other soldiers, do not perform Raiden's signature rolling kick, and keep the AKS-74u equipped at all times. If you do anything that's out of the ordinary for a guard and a fellow soldier notices, quickly change your behavior back to normal. Stand perfectly still and let the curious soldier examine you. After a moment, he will blow it off and return to his duties. If you run from a soldier that is asking you questions, he will sound the alarm. Just stay calm and play your cards right.

Navigation in Disguise

Dog Tags Can Wait

Now is not the time to obtain Dog Tags or take down guards. There will be a better time for this later, and full strategies will be described.

From the entrance, run under the surveillance camera and into the corridor. Quickly squeeze between the two guards patrolling here without letting either of them bump you. Move south (toward the screen), and follow the corridor to the center room.

300010

02001255

A box of **Chaff Grenades** is floating on some crates, and the local network Node is in the upper-right corner of the room. Download the map to the Soliton Radar, then search the lockers for items. In the south row of six lockers, you'll find **C4**, a **Book**, and **Claymores**. In the top-left row of three lockers, there are **M9 Bullets**. The top locker is locked. Punch the door until it falls off to reveal **M4 Bullets**.

Sexual Harassment

140.85 COLONEL

As you rest a moment in the 1F locker room, call the Colonel twice on the Codec. After he reminds you about not bumping into any guards with your disguise on, a rather funny scene occurs with Rose. If Rosemary previously agreed to look up information on Ames, she comes back with nothing—the person has no records whatsoever. A few more calls, and Rose will hint at the location of the Directional Microphone.

Nostalgic Moment

141.80 PLISKIN

Pliskin will elaborate on the AKS-74u and using it as part of a disguise. He hints that there may be a suppressor for the AK somewhere in the game. It would be extremely sweet to have a silenced machinegun! Another conversation has Pliskin kidding Raiden about the size of his suit and making an unmistakable reference to *Metal Gear Solid*.

8702001598010100214003B7

400110731

Proper **Identification**

Leave the locker area through the west door, and head up the corridor past the single guard and the surveillance camera. On the left side of this corridor is a small diversion, which used to be the west exit from Shell 1 before Fortune demolished it. **Socom Bullets** are by the door.

Move to the elevator and press ⃝. The camera scans Raiden's terrorist uniform and permits him access. If he doesn't have the uniform or the AKS-74u equipped, the alarm will sound.

Board the elevator and press the B2 button. Going on the hint that Rose has given us, we're going to search the lowest level first for a Directional Microphone.

Shell 1 Core, **B2 Computer Room**

Shell 1 Core B2 Computer Room

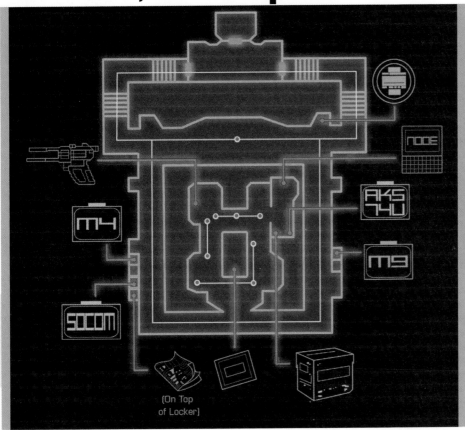

(On Top of Locker)

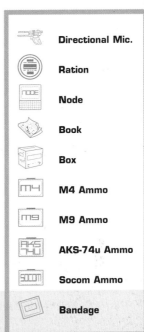

🔫	**Directional Mic.**
⬡	**Ration**
node	**Node**
📄	**Book**
📦	**Box**
m4	**M4 Ammo**
m9	**M9 Ammo**
AKS 74u	**AKS-74u Ammo**
socom	**Socom Ammo**
⬡	**Bandage**

Ride the elevator down to B2 first. Even though you've been instructed to search the B1 level for Ames, you'll first need some essential equipment.

Move down the east stairs toward the Computer Room, which is a heavily guarded area. One guard patrols the outside of the technician's area, and sometimes he will move around the square as if he is running laps. Be wary of his varying patterns and stay out of his way to avoid discovery. There's a **Ration** in the small alcove near the patrolling guard in the east area.

Move down the east corridor outside the computer area, and search the first locker on the right for **M9 Bullets**. Continue down and left into the technician's area. The **Directional Microphone** is located in the northwest corner of the computer area, near the squawking parrot. Move to the right, squeezing past the patrolling guard. The local network Node is in the northeast alcove. Download the map of the area and collect the **AKS-74u Bullets** and the **Cardboard Box 4**, which looks like a crate of McFarlane Toys. A **Bandage** is hidden under the central control panel. To take it, position Raiden on the east side of the center control panel. Wait until no guards are around, then crouch and crawl under the table to get it. Carefully watch the radar, and don't emerge until the coast is completely clear.

The four lockers in the west hallway also have items. **Socom Bullets** are in the second from the bottom, and **M4 Bullets** are in the last locker on the right.

Computer Room Nuances

There are several interesting things to watch in this area. The Policenauts *poster is hard to miss, and there are also* Zone of the Enders *and* Metal Gear Solid: Ghost Babel *posters near the Node. The parakeet is also fun to watch. The bird will become more conversational if you stand nearby and stare at it in First Person View. The guard who patrols the lower route is moving from one active console to another. Use First Person View to look over his shoulder when he is at either console. He is just surfing the Internet for hot girls!*

Shell 1 Core, B1

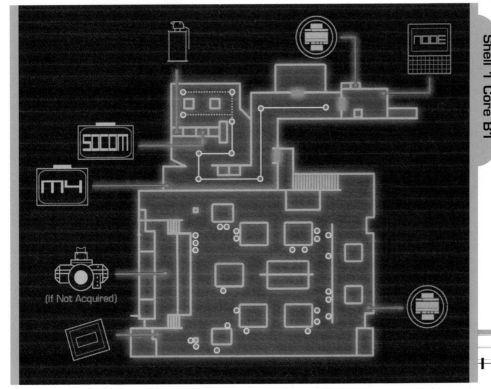

Shell 1 Core B1

Ration	
Stun Grenades	
Node	
Thermal goggles	
Bandage	
Socom Ammo	
M4 Ammo	

(If Not Acquired)

2 0 0 2 0 0 1 5 1 9 3 7 1 0 0 2 1 4 0 5

Exiting the elevator, Raiden spots a soldier using the retinal scanner to enter the hostage area. From there, enter the room to the right of the elevator. Inside, download the map of the area from the local network Node, and find the **Ration** stowed in the right side locker.

In the corridor, avoid any guards and navigate to the southwest corner, to find a box of **M4 Bullets**. The other guards don't mind if you do a little looting, as long as you stay in uniform. Search the lockers inside the break room for **Stun Grenades** and **Socom Bullets**.

Move outside the break room into the southwest corner of the corridor, and watch what the guards in this area are doing. One will leave the break room and patrol the corridor. When he returns and declares "All Clear," he will move to a position inside the break room and remain still, while another guard moves out to inspect the hall. The three men take turns patrolling in this manner.

The Retina Scanner

To fool the retina scanner system on the door into the hostage area, Raiden must sneak up on a guard, grab him in a chokehold, and drag him to the scanner. The best strategy is to wait in the southwest corner of the room for a guard to emerge from the break room. As he heads toward the scanner, unequip the AKS-74u and run up behind him. Stop directly behind the guard when he pauses in his route, and grab him in a chokehold by pressing and holding ⬜. Drag the guard toward the scanner. If the guard begins to struggle, just tap ⬜ once or twice. When Raiden's back touches the scanner, rotate the left stick so that he turns around and the guard faces the scanner. Then Raiden will shove the guard's face into the device, and the door will open.

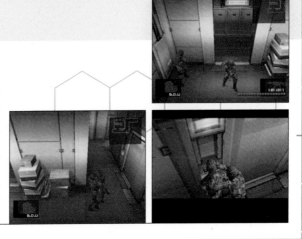

Handle With Care

If you choke the guard for too long, he will pass out. When he comes to, he will sound an alarm. If you accidentally break the guard's neck, then you have lost your opportunity. The movement of the other two guards is dependent upon the patrolling guard's return, and there's no way you can attack and choke one of the guards in the break room while another one is present. If the guard you're trying to use on the scanner passes out or dies, you will save time by running to the elevator and going to B2. Then return to B1, and everything will be reset for another attempt.

The Hostages

As you descend into the room where the hostages are held, make sure the B.D.U. and the AKS-74u are equipped. There is one patrolling guard in the hold, who reports in on his radio. Do not attempt to overthrow this guard—an alarm sounds automatically. There's a **Ration** against the wall on the far-left side of the room, and there's a **Bandage** below the podium on the right side of the room. If you didn't find the **Thermal Goggles** previously, they will be behind the podium on the stage.

This is how to look for Ames: When the guard is patrolling the other side of the room, equip the Directional Microphone and point it at the various hostages. If the guard spots Raiden with the Directional Microphone, he will immediately sound the alert.

Since Ames wears an electronic pacemaker, you need to listen for an electronic beep that accompanies the person's heartbeat. Once you have found Mr. Ames, press the Action button [△] to address him. If you address the wrong person, they will become scared and cry out. This will draw the attention of the other guard, so equip your AKS-74u and don't look suspicious. Either run away before the guard gets to where you are, or stand there and don't move while the guard asks you a bunch of questions before giving up. If you can't determine which hostage is Ames, the answer is at the end of this section.

The Hand of the La-li-lu-le-lo

AMES

Ames informs Raiden that the President is on the first floor of Shell 2. He also explains how the terrorists' nuclear button works. As long as the President is unwilling to input the codes, the computer will recognize this and refuses the input. Then the system must confirm the President's life signs via nanomachines or it will abort. Ames also has a bunch of answers to questions that Raiden didn't know to ask.

Private Conversations

Raiden then overhears a conversation between Ocelot and the terrorist leader, Solid Snake. During the scene where you listen in with the microphone, move it back and forth to hear each person better, or position it directly between them to hear both equally. The subtitle font size is at its largest when the signal is at its strongest.

Johnny Sasaki Returns!

During the scene in which Raiden listens to Ocelot and the terrorist leader, move the microphone toward the Lavatory to the left of the control room. Someone is having a pretty rough time in the restroom. Listen to his story carefully, and you'll realize that he's the poor guard everyone kept knocking out in Metal Gear Solid.

Wrath of the **Ninja**

Ocelot is coming! Ames gives Raiden the **Lv3 PAN Card**. He wants you to use it to reach Shell 2, where the President is held on the first floor. You have 10 seconds to equip your AKS-74U. Don't move! Just stand there innocently, or Ocelot will know!

Just when Ocelot has Raiden cornered, the Cyborg Ninja comes to the rescue. Although Raiden has escaped Revolver's torture device for now, he is now a hunted man throughout Shell 1.

Ames is the hostage at the bottom of the room, facing the south wall, leaning against the table with the boxes marked TDV-900HG. He's the only hostage with a unique hairstyle!

Shell 1 Core, **B1**

Raiden no longer has the Balaclava facemask, so the costume is now useless. Caution mode is in effect, so the patrol patterns of the guards have changed. Move toward the elevator. The guard patrolling here is really easy to get the drop on. It's time to start taking on guards and collecting Dog Tags, so read the three sections of tactics that follow for expert advice.

Do not return to 1F until the caution alert has been canceled. If you go up to 1F while security is this tight, an attack team member will be patrolling outside the corridor. Raiden will very likely have to take on the whole floor if he is discovered. Although blasting your way out of Shell 1 can be enthralling, don't take risky chances.

Shell 1 Core, **B1 Tactics**

Leaving this level or hiding until the Caution Alert is over isn't a difficult thing to do. Just move toward the elevator and wait until the guard looks the other way. Tranquilize him and stuff him into a locker in the nearby room, then wait there for the alert to end. Once the coast is clear, ride the elevator back up to 1F.

DOG TAG: Shell 1, B1 Elevator Guard
Difficulty: Easy

This guard patrols the space in front of the elevator only while the Caution Alert remains in effect, so you have to move on him swiftly. Position Raiden just around the corner from the guard; press Raiden's back flat against the wall. When the guard turns and heads east, run down the corridor and catch him just outside the door of the eastern Node room.

DOG TAG: Shell 1, B1 Lower Corridor Guard

DOG TAG: Shell 1, B1 Lower Corridor Guard

Difficulty: Easy

This guard will patrol the lower corridor only when the Caution Alert is still in effect, so you must move on him quickly. Position Raiden around the corner from the east end of the guard's route, with your back pressed flat against the wall. When the guard turns and starts to move west, quickly run around the corner and catch him.

DOG TAG: Shell 1, B1 Break Room Guard

Difficulty: Hard

Press Raiden's back up against the front of the lockers and knock. As the sentry comes to investigate the noise, run into the corridor and hide on the east side of the doorway, well out of the soldier's view. As he stares at the lockers, charge in and arrest him.

Shell 1 Core, **B2** Computer Room

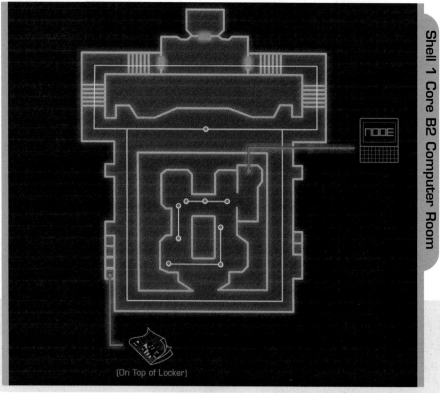

(On Top of Locker)

Shell 1 Core B2 Computer Room

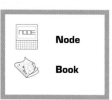

Node

Book

Now you can start collecting Dog Tags from the soldiers here. The challenge to get each of these guards alone in this wide-open space is very amusing. Save your game beforehand, because you will probably need a few tries.

DOG TAG: Shell 1, B2 Outer Perimeter Guard

Difficulty: Easy to Medium

The guard who patrols outside the control area is the easiest to catch. Just wait at the top of the stairs for him to turn and head west, then catch him. If the guard is patrolling quickly around the area as if he's running laps, then hide in one of the tiny spaces by the lockers in either of the side corridors. When the guard runs past, jump out and aim at the exact moment that he is directly in front of Raiden's position. This is a little trickier, but still not as tough as the three guards inside the control area.

DOG TAG: Shell 1, B2 Net Surfing Guard

Difficulty: Very Hard

The guard who patrols from monitor to monitor, looking at hot girls on the Internet, is the easiest target of the three. First, move to the southwest corner outside the computer room. Equip a naughty Book, and lay it in the southwest corridor. Try to place it a short distance from the wall, but far enough out that Raiden can run around the corner and get behind the guard.

Once the Book is placed, move to the lower wall and press Raiden's back against it. When the guard is surfing the net on the south computer, knock on the wall at the corner to draw his attention. As he comes outside to the point where Raiden knocked, run around the corner and stand out of view. The guard will spot the Book on the floor and move over to it. When you see the guard's cone of vision disappear from the radar, move out from the corner and capture him. Squeeze between the guard and the wall. After he gives up the tags, crouch and shoot a dart into his chin to knock him out.

DOG TAG: Shell 1, B1 West Computer Area Guard

Difficulty: Hard

Once you have used the net-surfing guard's vices against him, wait for the guard who patrols north to south on the west side of the computer area to move south. Run in front of the doorway from west to east, so that the guard sees your movement. Hide around the corner as the guard comes out to investigate. As soon as the guard's cone of vision returns to white

and he heads back, run around the corner and try to capture him outside the computer area. Once you have the tags and have tranquilized him, drag the body back outside the computer area, behind the partition.

DOG TAG: Shell 1, B1 North Computer Area Guard

Difficulty: Hard

After taking down every other guard in this area, move into the computer area and flatten Raiden's back against the *Policenauts* poster. When the guard is facing east or south at the east end of his route closest to the Node, knock on the poster. As the guard moves to investigate the noise, run around the central consoles and get behind the guard. Before he dismisses the sound and turns back, capture him!

Shell 1 Core, 1F

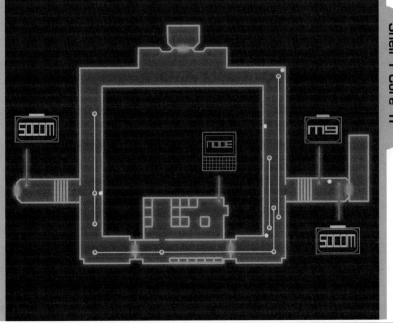

Shell 1 Core 1F

NODE	**Node**	
SOCOM	**Socom Ammo**	
M9	**M9 Ammo**	

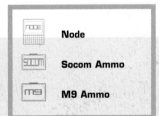

9 7 0 0 1 2 3 6

Do not return to this corridor until the Caution Alert previously invoked by Ocelot has ended. If you return to this level too soon, there are too many soldiers to deal with. But after the alert ends, the attack team will leave.

Getting down the corridor is tricky. Take out cameras with the suppressed Socom, and knock out the soldiers with the M9. If you want to collect Dog Tags, the Alert must be absolutely over. Now is the time to do it.

In the east exit corridor, use the Socom to knock out the camera while Raiden is still standing inside the hallway. **Socom Bullets** and **M9 Bullets** are below the camera.

DOG TAG: Shell 1, 1F Northeast Corridor Guard

Difficulty: Medium

The first soldier to take out is the one who patrols the north part of the east corridor, and occasionally turns left and patrols near the elevator. Use the Socom with the silencer to knock out the camera in the northeast corner. Then move to the corner's edge and flatten your back against it. When the solider stops at the northeast corner of his route, step away from the wall, nudge the left stick toward the guard a bit and surprise him. There should be plenty of room to squeeze between the guard and the wall to demand his Dog Tags. After putting the guard to sleep, drag his body just around the corner to hide it.

DOG TAG: Shell 1, 1F West Corridor Guard

Difficulty: Medium

After taking down the northeast corner guard, move to the west corridor and position Raiden at the top corner. When the guard is patrolling the south end of his route, step out and use the Socom to destroy the surveillance camera. Then hide behind the corner until the guard stops at the north end of his route. When the guard turns back and starts south, run down the corridor and catch him as quickly as possible.

DOG TAG: Shell 1, 1F South Guard

Difficulty: Medium

This soldier appears only when Raiden is leaving Shell 1. He patrols through the locker room on the south side of the area, and emerges into the hallways on either side. Having taken out the guard in the west corridor, wait until this guard emerges from the locker room on the west side. Then follow him into the locker room, where he stops just a few feet into the door. Capture him there before he moves too far east.

DOG TAG: Shell 1, 1F Southwest Corner Guard

Difficulty: Medium

Having overtaken both the guard who patrols the locker room and the guard who monitors the northeast corner, this guard should become a little easier. Step just outside the east door of the locker room, and aim the Socom at the camera high on the corner. It's a bit easier to hit when it's searching the south. Just make sure that the guard isn't nearby when the camera fizzles out, or he will spot Raiden very quickly. Once the camera is out, press Raiden's back to the corner and wait for the guard to come south. When he turns and heads back north, run around the corner and up behind him to catch him unawares.

MISSION 04: THE CROSSING

Going on the information divulged by Colonel Ames, Raiden must now blaze a path to Shell 2. As the terrorist leader Solid Snake indicated, the Shell 1-2 Bridge is wired with IR sensor beams and Semtex explosives set to go off when anything crosses the beams. To eliminate all of the explosives efficiently and cross the bridge, Raiden must find a sniper rifle. Perhaps the Lv3 PAN Card Ames gave to Raiden will be helpful.

EF Connecting Bridge

Just inside the Shell 1 doorway, stop and wait for three Gun Cyphers to come into view. Take out all three with the silenced Socom, since there is a guard standing lookout at the top of the Heliport's stairs. After all the Gun Cyphers explode, carefully target the lookout guard with the M9. It's difficult to manage from this angle with the sun in your eyes, but keep adjusting until you hear the guard choke and drop. Then return to Strut F.

Strut F **Warehouse**

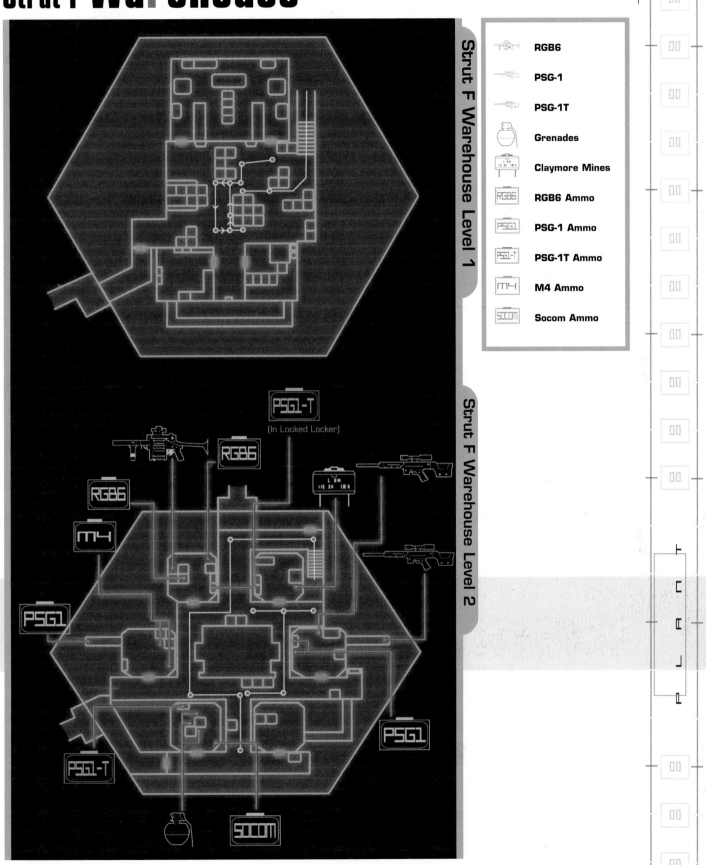

RGB6

PSG-1

PSG-1T

Grenades

Claymore Mines

RGB6 RGB6 Ammo

PSG1 PSG-1 Ammo

PSG1-T PSG-1T Ammo

M4 M4 Ammo

SOCOM Socom Ammo

PSG1-T
(In Locked Locker)

RGB6

RGB6

M4

PSG1

PSG1-T

PSG1

SOCOM

With Colonel Ames' Lv3 PAN Card, Raiden can now ransack the remaining rooms in the Strut F Warehouse. Use the same tactics described previously to take the guards out of the equation. New **Claymores** have appeared in the northeast Lv2 room.

Two boxes of **M4 Bullets** have appeared in the middle Lv2 room on the west side. Remember that there are **PSG-1 Bullets** in the crawlspace as before. Raiden finally finds the **PSG-1 Sniper Rifle** and a box of **Bullets** for it in the middle Lv3 room to the east. More **PSG-1 Bullets** are in the locker. The **PSG-1T**, a sniper rifle that fires tranquilizer darts, is in a crawl-space on the east side of the room. Since bullets for this gun are so rare, save all that you can get for later events.

In the northwest Lv3 room, Raiden will find the **RGB6 Grenade Launcher** and two boxes of **RBG6 Grenades**. Although optional, this weapon makes a certain upcoming boss fight much easier. There is a locked locker that contains **PSG-1T Bullets**, if you can punch off the door. These are extremely rare to find, so don't forget that they are here.

The Lv3 room by the FA Connecting Bridge contains a much-needed box of **Socom Bullets**, three boxes of **Grenades**, and **PSG-1T Bullets** are in the locker.

EF Connecting Bridge

Use the PSG-1 to eliminate the lookout at the top of the Heliport stairs. Then switch over to the Socom and take out the two or three Gun Cyphers by aiming for the gun on their undersides.

Strut D

Remember that there are **PSG-1 Bullets** by the EF Connecting Bridge entrance. Equip the M9 and tranquilize the guards on the central bridge, then grab the bullets and enter the door on the north side, which leads to the Shell 1-2 Connecting Bridge.

Shell 1-2 Connecting Bridge

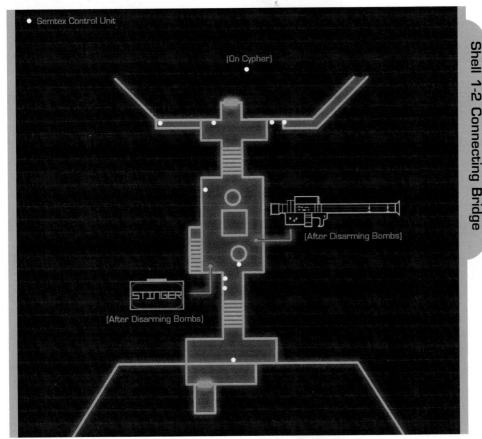

- Semtex Control Unit
- (On Cypher)
- (After Disarming Bombs)
- STINGER (After Disarming Bombs)

	Stinger
STINGER	**Stinger Ammo**

Pliskin finally contacts Raiden after a long silence, explaining how Raiden must shoot all the control units to disengage the infrared sensors on the bridge. Call Pliskin again and he explains that you need a sniper rifle. He also tells you where to get one if you don't have it.

Sniping Basics

Becoming an expert sniper overnight doesn't just happen, but Raiden must adapt quickly if he is to move on. When you equip the PSG-1, Raiden instantly shifts to scope view. As you look through the scope, press ⚪ to zoom in, ✖ to zoom out, and ⚫ to fire. The closer you zoom to an object, the harder it is to miss. Aiming is quicker when you look in the general direction of the target in First Person View beforehand. To aim more accurately, use a Pentazemin to steady your hands. The Pentazemin lasts only about one minute, so keep them handy. Finally, laying down on the ground will help stabilize your aim.

Since there are no live targets in this situation, you shouldn't need to use more than one Pentazemin. You can shoot most of the C4 control boxes with just the Socom anyhow.

To the right is a list of the control boxes you can hit with the Socom. Take these out first:

A control box is directly above Raiden's location over the doorway. This is the easiest Socom shot.

One is attached to the small, white-striped pump a few feet beyond the beams. Raiden views it with his scope during the previous scene. This is the second easiest Socom shot.

There are two control boxes nestled on the left side of the bridge among C4 packs and the IR beams. Shoot the white tops of them to avoid hitting the C4.

This section shows the C4 control boxes that are easier to hit with the PSG-1 sniper rifle:

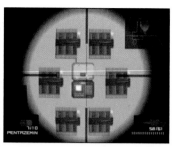

Move directly to the left of the Strut D doorway. Equip the PSG-1 and zoom in on the Sons of Liberty flag on the far left. Eventually, the breeze will flap it out far enough to reveal the control box behind it. After you get a glimpse, estimate its location in relation to the flag, and fire.

From the same position left of the Strut D doorway, look directly ahead. Some birds are clustered around a control box below the Strut G entrance. Fire a warning shot to make the birds scatter. If that doesn't work, you may have to shoot one. Then shoot the box.

Another one is further up the same wall, snuggled in the middle of six C4 bundles. Zoom in extremely close to it and fire.

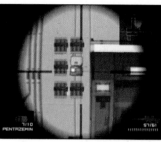

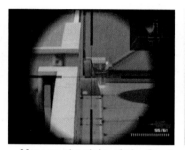

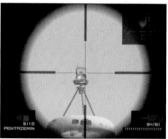

Just to the left of the Strut G entrance, a control box is nestled among five C4 bundles. Zoom in extremely close and shoot.

Move to the right of the Strut D doorway, and look down at the bridge. A control box is on the floor of the bridge at the other end. You can only see its profile. Zoom in extremely close on the box to avoid hitting the Semtex behind it. Target the top portion just to be safe.

The last one is attached to the top of a Cypher that's moving in a triangular pattern over Strut G. Zoom in extremely close and follow the Cypher to one of the corners of its path. Make sure you hit the control box and not the camera to which it is mounted, or the Cypher will emit a signal and destroy the bridge!

Grunt Sniping Technique

141.80

PLISKIN

While it's good to be back in contact with Pliskin after a long period of silence, his advice about sniper techniques is somewhat grouchy! To supplement the sniper tips we've provided, contact Pliskin as much as you desire for seemingly endless "sniper dos and don'ts." Plus, if you shoot all the other control boxes and then view the Cypher above Strut G with the Scope, Pliskin calls and chides you out for missing the one on the Cypher—what a pill!

Enter Solidus

After you hear the IR beams shut off, run onto the bridge and receive a call from Pliskin. The surly SEAL has found a Kasatka, and the two devise a plan on how to get the hostages off the Big Shell. As Pliskin and his pal approach in the helicopter, the menacing figure who calls himself Solid Snake emerges. Unfortunately, Pliskin finds himself divulging more than he planned!

SOLIDUS SNAKE

The shadowy figure known by the codename "Solidus" is the third of three super-soldiers created in the "Les Enfants Terrible" project, a genetic cloning experiment designed to reproduce an enhanced clone of the greatest soldier ever known, Big Boss. Only now is Solidus stepping out from the shadows, remaining on the sidelines during the previous events in Outer Heaven, Zanzibar, and Shadow Moses Island. Solidus was once the President of the United States, under the assumed name George Sears. He sent his most trusted agent, Revolver Ocelot, to incite Liquid Snake to start the uprising at Shadow Moses. When Solid Snake interfered in Solidus's plans to capture Metal Gear REX, he was forced to resign from the Presidency by the shadowy organization known as the Patriots. Since then, he has been spearheading the activities of Dead Cell, the anti-terrorist training squad that he assembled during his term.

SOLIDUS SNAKE   (John Cygan)

AV-88 Harrier II

Pilot	Solidus Snake
Weapons:	AIM-9 Sidewinders; AGM-65 Maverick Missiles; GAU-12 25MM Six-Barrel Gun Pod, 300 Round Capacity with Lead Computing Optical Sight System (LCOSS)

Grab the **Stinger Launcher** and the box of **Stinger Missiles** Pliskin throws down. Be sure to equip the Rations so that Raiden can hopefully survive severe damage. Throughout the battle, if Raiden runs low on Rations, Pliskin will throw down more from the chopper. Don't hit the Kastaka with a Stinger by mistake, or the free items will stop coming. If the Kasataka is destroyed, the game ends. Be ready to click off the Stinger at any moment by tapping L2 . Raiden has to be able to run and dodge attacks, and at some points in the battle, this is more important than targeting the Harrier II.

Now examine the Soliton Radar and note the positions of both the Harrier II and the Kasatka on the radar. The fighter jet is the big red arrow and the Kasatka is the small red dot. Turn Raiden to face the general direction of the Harrier II, then equip the Stinger. In normal view, the Stinger will analyze your target's weak points and mark them in its radar eyepiece as small squares, even at extremely long range. Align the center crosshairs on that square, and the Stinger will lock onto the target. Fire, and the missile will fly after that target until the rocket runs out of fuel. To quickly remove the Stinger's scope from your eye, press and hold R1 . This helps if you are worried about attacks from the side. The Stinger can still track targets via sonar in this mode.

When the Stinger draws a bead on the Harrier and the fighter jet is in the open, fire. If the Harrier is circling around, the missile will follow it for a while and then fall away. During the first course of the battle, Solidus flies the Harrier some distance away, then soars in and buzzes the bridge. Raiden will be knocked off his feet and take damage if this happens, so find the target quickly and launch a Stinger. When the Harrier is charging and a missile hits it, the jet is knocked off course and must abort the attack run. Solidus will also try to hurt Raiden with heat from the Harrier's jets. Simply aim the Stinger anywhere at the fighter's underbelly and fire. You'll inflict more damage if you can target one of the highlighted areas in the Stinger's scope, but the most important thing is to drive off the Harrier before its exhaust jets cause Raiden too much pain.

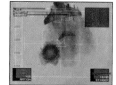

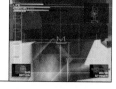

After it loses a quarter of its stamina, the Harrier will release a volley of missiles. The best thing you can do is run toward Strut D, because the entire middle section of the bridge will be blasted out. Generally, Raiden cannot seem to outrun this particular attack. However, anytime the Harrier releases missiles after this, just drop off any edge to the level below and hide behind the pumps and pipes. The downside is that there is hardly any way to attack from this level, so when the Harrier moves off, run back up to the top level. If the Harrier closes in while Raiden is emerging from below, it will pin him down with machinegun fire. After a few minutes of this, Pliskin radios that he will take care of it and fires a grenade at the plane just to drive it off. If you stay under cover when the Harrier tries to pin you down, Pliskin will help you out every time.

When the Harrier dips below the bridge, it will rise, and Solidus will attempt to hit Raiden with gunfire. The Stinger will display four targets under the plane, so just move the crosshairs left or right until the Stinger locks onto one. After you fire that missile, try to lock onto another target and fire.

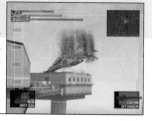

The most important key to winning this battle is to rely on the Soliton Radar. Constantly monitor the Harrier's position on the radar, and keep changing Raiden's position to better see it through the Stinger's scope. If the Harrier flies from one side of the bridge to the other, unequip the Stinger, turn, and equip it again. This is faster than turning in First Person View. Continue chipping away at the Harrier until you prevail.

AV-8B HARRIER II

Equipped with the combat-proven APG-65 radar system, the Harrier II provides improved self-defense and pilot situational awareness. The engine is an increased-thrust version of the Rolls-Royce Pegasus F402-RR-408. The Harrier II was developed through a three-nation agreement among the United States, Spain and Italy. The Boeing Company, British Aerospace and Rolls-Royce teamed together to produce the AV-8B, an upgrade from the AV-8A.

Armaments of the Harrier II series include seven external store stations, comprising six wing stations for AIM-9 Sidewinder missiles and an assortment of air-to-ground weapons, external fuel tanks, and AGM-65 Maverick missiles. A GAU-12 25MM six-barrel gun pod can be mounted on the centerline under the nose, and it has a 300 round capacity with a lead-computing optical sight system (LCOSS).

Treacherous Passage

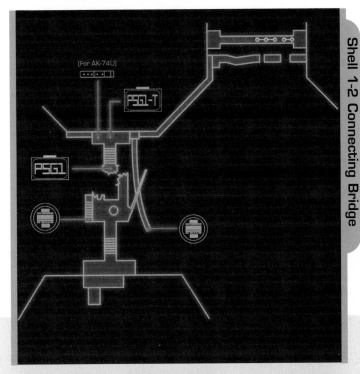

Shell 1-2 Connecting Bridge

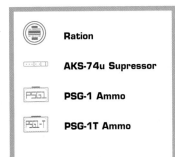

	Ration
	AKS-74u Supressor
	PSG-1 Ammo
	PSG-1T Ammo

300010

The Shell 1-2 bridge is on fire and in pieces. Move left to the burning area, and the Cell Phone will start to ring and buzz. Equip the Cell Phone to receive an email from the Ninja. Use the Coolant to put out the fire, then quickly run down the stairs to get a **Ration**. Quickly run back up, before Raiden falls into the ocean with the collapsing stairs.

Move to the right railing, leap over it, and hang. Shimmy out until it seems Raiden is directly over the orange pipe below. Use First Person View to confirm your position directly over the pipe, then drop down. Carefully work your way back along the pipe toward Strut D, where you will find another **Ration** at the end. Now carefully move back to where you were.

When you reach the first gob of bird droppings on the pipe, move slowly or crawl around this area so that Raiden doesn't slip off and fall. Just past that area, stand and face left. Use First Person View to line up perfectly with the platform opposite your position. Raiden can do his amazing torso-axial jump over to the left platform. There are **PSG-1 Bullets** on the left edge of this dangling gantry. Move up to the doorway and use the Coolant again to put out the fire blocking access to the **AKS-74u Suppressor**—now you have a silenced machinegun! **PSG-1T Bullets** are nearby.

Head left and drop onto the platform where the pipe connects. Press ○ to pull yourself up onto the walkway. As Raiden moves around the outside of Strut G, the catwalk begins to fall apart. Keep running until you reach the end. If you want to go back for any reason, Raiden can do torso-axial jumps to get across the new gaps. It's too tricky to attempt, so make sure you don't need to go back.

At the top of the narrow catwalk, flip over the rail and hang. Drop to the catwalk below. Two soldiers will emerge on the bridge above. Use the sniper rifle to take them out. Make sure neither one gets the chance to radio in, or you'll become a sitting duck. Do a torso-axial jump over the first gap. At the second gap, jump over the rail and hang, then shimmy across to the end. Climb the ladder at the end.

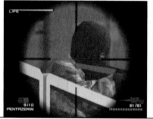

Strut L Perimeter

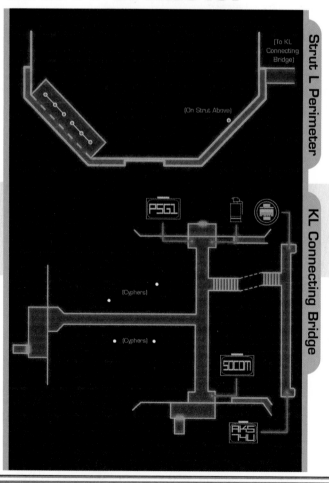

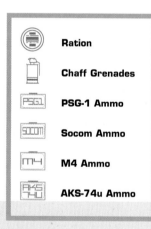

Ration	
Chaff Grenades	
PSG-1 Ammo	
Socom Ammo	
M4 Ammo	
AKS-74u Ammo	

Two guards will move from window to window, looking out over the catwalk. If they spot Raiden, they will radio for a few Gun Cyphers to come take him out. Crouch, press Raiden's back against the wall, and sidestep under the windows. When part of the catwalk threatens to give, go back instead of forward. Crouch under the window if a guard is about to pass. When the nearest guard is walking, jump over the rail and hang. Shimmy to the right until you can't go any further. Watch the guards in the windows; when they are far enough away and walking, jump back onto the platform. Crouch immediately and hide from the soldiers by pressing Raiden's back against the wall. Continue crouch-stepping under the windows.

After the windows comes a gap that is too long to jump over. Press Raiden's back against the wall and sidestep across the gap using the thin ledge. Careful, though—if Raiden steps out from the wall, he'll fall off. When you get to the obstruction, just crouch and continue under it.

Nature Calls

Past the long gap, a guard above your position decides he has to go to the restroom and just can't wait. The only question is, will you waste your time waiting for him to finish, or will you just hold your breath and run under it? Actually, you have another option or two. You can flip over the rail, hang, and then shimmy along the edge. Or, you can fire a shot at the platform on which the guard stands; this might startle him enough to make him pause.

Once you've crossed under this guard, you should use First Person View or a Corner View and look around. You can't miss spotting the small fleet of Gun Cyphers hovering above the KL Connecting Bridge. Use the silenced AKS-74u to take them out. Press ⬤ lightly to aim the weapon with laser sighting, and then press harder to fire. Drop over the rail and grab the **AKS-74u Bullets**. There's a **Ration** at the other side of this path. Climb up the stairs. There are **PSG-1 Bullets** and **Chaff Grenades** near Strut K's malfunctioning entrance. You'll find **Socom Bullets** near Strut K.

To cross the damaged bridge to Shell 2, do a torso-axial jump over the first gap. At the second gap, press Raiden against the upper railing and sidestep across.

Codec Chat Time

140.85

COLONEL

Talk to the Colonel as you stand at the windows. He offers advice about using the Stun Grenade preemptively on the guards. Rose will offer to dig up additional information on Vamp. And surprisingly, the Colonel refuses to believe that Solid Snake is now involved in the mission. In spite of their previously strong friendship, Campbell doesn't believe that Raiden should trust Snake with this important mission.

The Real Snake

141.85

SNAKE

Raiden gets Snake to admit who he really is and to talk about the meaning behind his alias. Snake isn't any less gruff about the matter than he usually is, however. The various communications also touch on Solidus's mention of Outer Heaven, and Snake recalls Ames's connection to Nastasha Romanenko.

MISSION 05: PRESIDENTIAL RESCUE

As he enters the Shell 2 Core, Raiden watches as Olga Gurlukovich electrifies the floor in front of the room where the President is being held. This brief mission involves knocking out the electric current in order to reach the President of the United States.

Shell 2 Core, 1F Air Purification Room

`1024013295000`

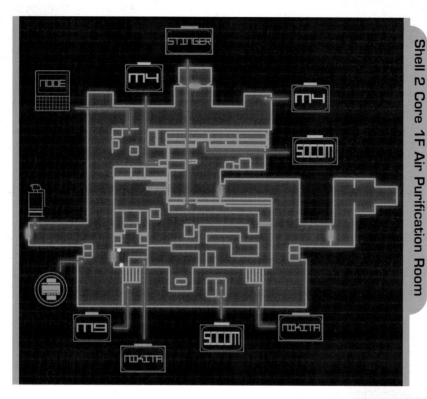

Shell 2 Core 1F Air Purification Room

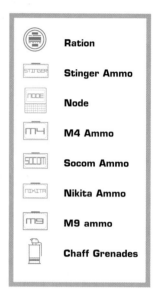

Ration	
Stinger Ammo	
Node	
M4 Ammo	
Socom Ammo	
Nikita Ammo	
M9 ammo	
Chaff Grenades	

Raiden overhears a conversation between Olga and Solidus. Move the Directional Microphone to follow Olga as she paces in order to hear the conversation better. Afterward, a section of floor is electrified outside the room where the President is being held. The Colonel and Rose call to offer advice.

What a Shocker!

If you're not short on health and want a really good laugh, go ahead and step on the electric floor. Wiggle the Left Analog Stick to break free from the shock.

Nikita Location

Call Snake to find out the location of a Nikita Rocket Launcher on B1 of the Shell 2 Core. Sounds like you'll have a little swimming to do...

97001236

`02001255`

124 PART 2 PLANT

Finding the Nikita

Move down the stairs to the west and notice the two holes in the north wall. These vents will be utilized later. Hop onto the box for **Socom Bullets** if you need them. The Nikita Rockets will have to wait for a while. Continue left to find **M9 Bullets**, and go upstairs.

There's a **Ration** at the top of the stairs. Step close enough to the door across the hall to open it but don't go inside; two Gun Cameras are mounted above, on the other side of the threshold. Use the Socom to shoot them out. There are more Nikita Rockets in here, but again, you need the firing mechanism first.

Continuing north, diverge into the left corridor to find **Chaff Grenades** near the malfunctioning west exit. Looks like you won't be able to get to the HL Connecting Bridge this way. Continue north in the corridor until you find a small employee break area. Pick up **M4 Bullets** and login to the local Node.

Hail to the Chief

Now press up against the east wall of the break area; the camera will shift to partially reveal the President's room. Knock on the wall, and he will respond. Continue knocking on the wall, and he will

remain there several minutes listening. Knock too rapidly, and he will get annoyed and walk off. Also, if you gaze upon the wall where you were knocking, you'll see a two-level map of the entire ventilation system on this floor.

Follow the northern corridor east past the elevator to reach some more **M4 Bullets**. Then take the elevator down to B1.

Shell 2 Core, B1 Filtration Chamber No. 1

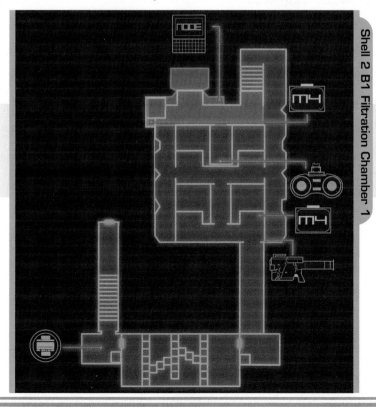

Shell 2 B1 Filtration Chamber 1

![Ration icon]	**Ration**
![Night Vision Goggles icon]	**Night Vision Goggles**
![M4 icon]	**M4 Ammo**
![Radio Guided Missile icon]	**Radio Guided Missile**
![Node icon]	**Node**

```
              2 0 0 1 5 9 8 0 1 0 1 0 0 2 1 4 0 0
     010      101      111      20      020
```

As you exit the elevator on B1, login to the Node and be thankful—this section requires you to swim underwater. The Colonel calls to remind Raiden of the swim controls.

When you're underwater, look for light spots on the floor or on the Soliton Radar map. These indicate air pockets directly above. Press ⬤ to swim, press the Left Analog Stick up to go up, down to go down, and right or left to turn either way. You can make hard turns with the Right Analog Stick— press right or left to turn 90° instantly, or press down to turn 180° degrees completely around.

From the point where you must submerge in order to continue, just swim directly forward until you find the **Nikita**. There are other underwater corridors to explore, but that will be more important when you come back. Return to the area on 1F where you saw the vent holes high in the wall.

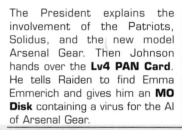

0159801056730011 0400   012033401

Shell 2 Core, 1F Air Purification Room

Move south past the President's room to the small, dark room with the Gun Cameras that you disabled. Step onto the block and grab the **Nikita Rockets**. Also, remember that there are more **Nikita Rockets** by the stairs where you saw the vent holes in the wall.

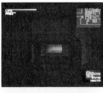

In the dark room with the Gun Cameras, step onto the block and face the vent on the opposite side of the room. Fire a Nikita into the vent, and guide it through the twists and turns into the President's room. Destroy the large circuit breaker in the northeast corner. If you want to slow down the missile, press left or right to change its direction a little. You can also use the vents by the stairs, but the vent in the Gun Camera room offers a duct path that's easier to navigate.

The President explains the involvement of the Patriots, Solidus, and the new model Arsenal Gear. Then Johnson hands over the **Lv4 PAN Card**. He tells Raiden to find Emma Emmerich and gives him an **MO Disk** containing a virus for the AI of Arsenal Gear.

This is Card 4. It'll give you access all the way to Emma's location.

After the scenes, search the President's room for **Socom Bullets**. There's a vent at floor level in the south wall. Climb in and grab the **Stinger Missiles**. As you leave the room, Raiden contacts the Colonel. He is ordered to find Emma and bring the MO Disk virus to the Shell 1 B2 Computer Room. Go back to the elevator and return to B1.

About Emma Emmerich

140.85
COLONEL

After you leave the President's cell, call Campbell on the Codec, and he will provide you with Emma Emmerich's entire life story, obtained from NSA files. If you requested information on Vamp, Rose will have it ready if you call again.

Miscommunication

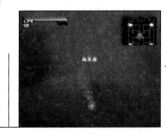

Call Snake's line a few times, and eventually Otacon will answer. He admits that he and Snake haven't exactly been up front with Raiden, and then the conversation takes a really amusing turn from there. Continue calling this line to get more information about the Metal Gear project from Otacon.

MISSION 06: THE CHILD GENIUS

Holding the virus contained on the MO Disk, Raiden needs to find the last living systems programmer on the Arsenal Gear project. The President said that Emma was rumored to be in captivity on the flooded B1 level. Only she can upload the virus to Arsenal Gear's system.

Shell 2 Core, B1 Filtration Chamber No. 1

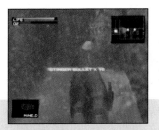

Swim to the place where you got the Nikita, and you'll find a new **Ration**. Return toward the entrance and swim west. Take the first left, and swim into the small area to find the **Night Vision Goggles**. Continue swimming west and catch a breath at the next skylight. Otacon should call you with some revelations about Emma's personality.

Swim south and take the next left. A sea mine floats in the center of this corridor. Using the Mine Detector, all the mines show up as little red dots on the radar. Touch them, and BOOM! Swim south from the first mine, and then swim to the left at the T-intersection. Find the **M4 Bullets** in the corner, then turn around and swim south again. Two mines float in the corridor. Carefully swim under the first mine and over the other. Don't move too quickly; just tap ⊙ occasionally so that Raiden swims slowly through here. When you reach the end, catch your breath in the skylight. Look beneath you in First Person View—there are two watertight doors. Following the Soliton's map, open the west door. Peter Stillman's body floats out, so this must be where he died.

In the room strewn with girders, there is a confusing maze to swim through. Reach the first skylight for some air, and then look around in First Person View to find the gap low in the girders. Swim to the south wall, and then left. Follow this opening until you see the light of the next skylight on the floor. You'll find more **Stinger Missiles** there. Continue swimming west to the watertight door and open it. The next room has a skylight, but a mine floats on the surface. Instead of getting air there, just swim to the right and go up the stairs to the exit.

BOSS FIGHT

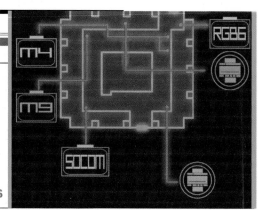

Vamp

Gender:	Male
Affiliation:	Dead Cell Knife Specialist
Weapon:	Throwing Knives, Serrated Hunting Knives

You've seen this guy in action, so you know that bullets are mostly ineffective. Equip the RGB6 and the Rations. Aim with First Person View and blast Vamp where he hovers over the water. He will swim around for some time. Do yourself a favor and equip the Socom whenever Vamp is underwater; blast out the lights all around the upper level of the room. Vamp will use an attack later on that is detrimental to your survival—he is capable of pinning Raiden's shadow to the floor with a knife. If his shadow is pinned, Raiden can't move. Then Vamp can hit Raiden with all the throwing knives he wants.

Socom Bullets, two boxes of **M4 Bullets**, a **Ration,** and a box of **RBG6 Shells** are positioned around the room. Except for the Rations, don't pick up these items until you absolutely need them. There's no use picking up a box of ammo if all you receive is one bullet.

After you first knock Vamp into the water, spend some time blowing out any remaining lights around the room with the Socom. Stand at the entrance to the room on the south side as you do this. When Vamp leaps out onto the lower level, equip the RGB6 and fire a grenade at him. Use First Person View, and be sure to raise your aim to compensate for the arcing trajectory of the shell. The force of the blast will blow Vamp back into the water, and the attack does tremendous damage. Stay at the entrance to the room to see what Vamp does next. If he leaps all the way up to the upper railing, start moving around the room. He will begin throwing clusters of knives at Raiden, and it's just better to concentrate on dodging for a round. Eventually Vamp will get tired of this, and he'll leap back into the water. During his next attack, he will most likely jump onto the lower platform. Position yourself by the entrance again, and aim at the same spot on the other side of the platform where he landed last time.

When Vamp is at 30% health or less, he will begin the aforementioned attack of pinning Raiden's shadow to the floor. Hopefully, you were smart enough to shoot out the lights before then. If the lower level is dark and Vamp cannot pin Raiden's shadow, he will go berserk and start flying wildly around the room, flinging knives from every angle. Just keep moving and dodging. Equip one of the machineguns and run in circles around the platform. Eventually, Vamp will land very near Raiden for a close-quarters attack. Blast him with the machinegun, and the battle should be over.

If you need an extra Ration, there is one floating near the north edge of the water. Flip over the northern rail and hang, then shimmy over to the item location. Vamp shouldn't be able to give you too much trouble while you're going for this item.

0132950010021486 0187

VAMP

$$OH - O \begin{array}{c} H \\ \\ O \end{array} P \begin{array}{c} \\ \\ C_4 \end{array}$$

Vamp is Romanian born. When he was very young, his entire family was wiped out when a terrorist bomb exploded in a church. Wounded and trapped in the rubble, Vamp was forced to feed on the blood of his own dead family members for three days before rescue workers found him. That is how he obtained his disgusting thirst for blood. Vamp is a member of Dead Cell due to his close relationships with Fortune and her deceased father, Marine Commandant Scott Dolph. Like the other members, he too once believed in preparing the armed forces for the war against terrorism. However, after his former commander and good friend Colonel Jackson was deposed, that view obviously changed. No one knows for sure the source of Vamp's powers, or how it is that he can live on after death. But Vamp is a terrifying foe and a worthy adversary.

VAMP (Phil La Marr)

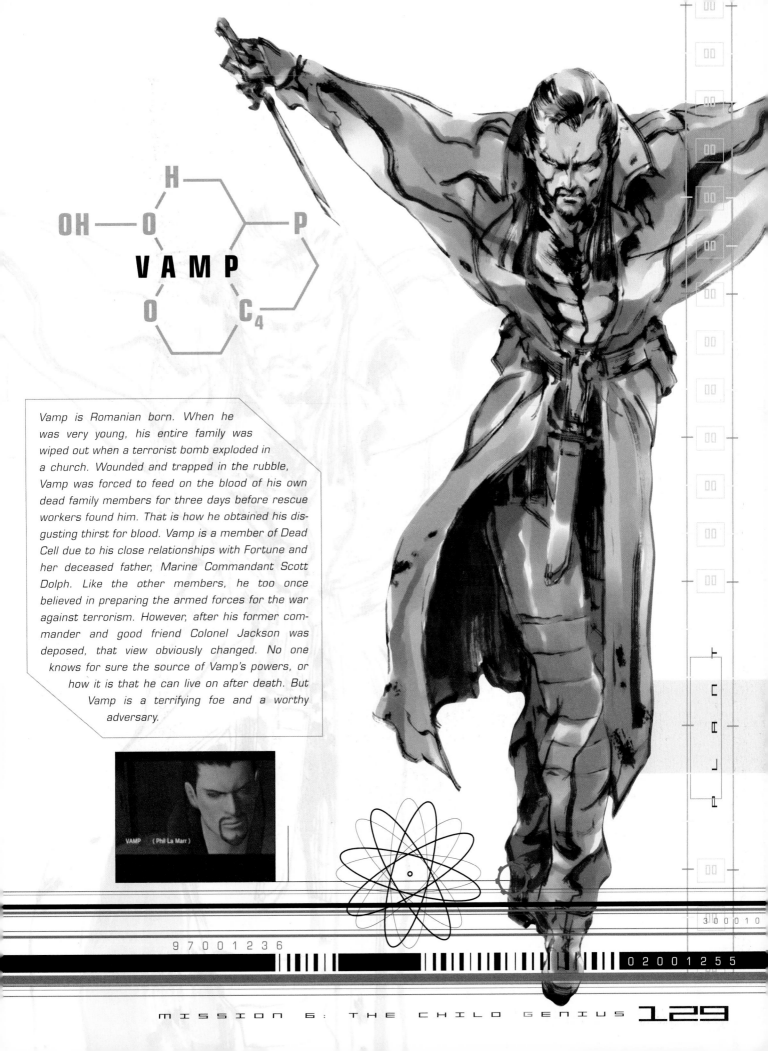

97 0 0 1 2 3 6

02 0 0 1 2 5 5

3 0 0 0 1 0

Shell 2 Core, B1 Filtration Chamber No. 2

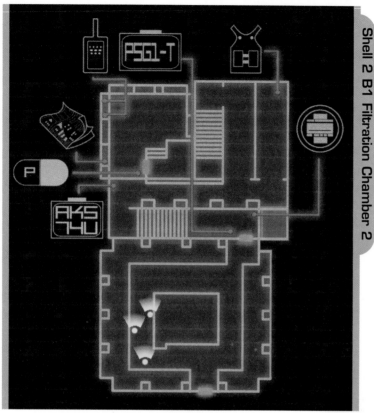

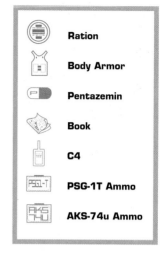

Legend:

- (Ration icon) **Ration**
- (Body Armor icon) **Body Armor**
- (Pentazemin icon) **Pentazemin**
- (Book icon) **Book**
- (C4 icon) **C4**
- (PSG-1T icon) **PSG-1T Ammo**
- (AKS-74u icon) **AKS-74u Ammo**

After the battle, grab whatever items are left in the room and proceed north. Grab the **Ration** in the hallway and descend the stairs into the water. Unfortunately, you don't have the Soliton Radar map of this section! However, if you equip the Mine Detector, you will be able to see the Node in this area as a little blue dot not too far away.

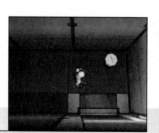

||||||||||||||||||||||| 4 2 3 0 1 0 3 0 0 5 5

Swimming straight ahead from the bottom of the steps, you'll enter a small room where there's a mine and a box of **AKS-74u Bullets**. Return to the corridor and catch a breath at the skylight. Enter First Person View, and Raiden will spot Emma Emmerich waiting in a small control room. Swim all the way to the end, where there are three doorways. At the end, swim to the left and under the mine to find the **Body Armor**. Across the hall, there are some **PSG-1T Bullets** in a room with two mines. Now get some air at the skylight. Look down in First Person at the two doorways, and swim through the one on the left. Climb the stairs and go into the control room.

Hide and Seek

Emma must be hiding in one of the lockers, because she's nowhere to be seen. Download the map from the Node and grab the **Pentazemin** sitting at the bottom of the steps. You can check to see if Emma is in a locker by knocking on it. She will let out a small yelp. Start with the locker on the far left, where you'll find another **Book**. There are two boxes of **C4** in the top-left locker. Emma is hiding in the center locker of the top row.

Emma is the younger sister of the brilliant Armstech engineer, Hal Emmerich, also known as "Otacon." Hal was the lead designer on the Metal Gear REX project and developer of the PAN Card Security system in the Shadow Moses facility and in Big Shell. Living in a family of great scientists and inventors, Emma feels that she has a great deal to live up to. Pushing her mind and computer skills past their limits, she has created an Artificial Intelligence (AI) and programmed it into the computer system of the massive new Metal Gear project named Arsenal Gear. The sibling rivalry that has always existed between Emma and Otacon has never abated, and even a crisis situation such as this is not enough to curb Emma's need to prove herself to her famous older brother.

EMMA EMMERICH

Emma's Return to **Swimming**

After the cut scenes, swim with Emma back to the room where Raiden fought Vamp, stopping at every skylight along the way for air. Emma's breath and life are too short to risk long swims. Once you're out of the water, press △ to make Emma grab Raiden's hand, then lead her into the next area.

Notes on Emma

When Emma is partnered with Raiden, there are several things to keep in mind. Press △ to make Emma take Raiden's hand. Raiden cannot hold a weapon or fight while he's holding Emma's hand. If you need to scout ahead, leave Emma in a safe place where enemies won't find her. If Emma's life meter is low, let her rest for a while. While Emma is sitting down, her life meter will recharge.

With the Mine Detector equipped, you can see that the west side of the chamber is full of **Claymores**. Don't lead Emma in that direction for any reason. If you do hit a mine, the Ninja will send you an email on the Cell Phone.

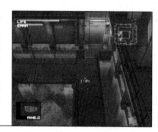

The Quarreling Geniuses

141.80

SNAKE/OTACON

In the room where you fought Vamp, contact this frequency several times to see the two smartest people on earth duke it out with their minds and a twinge of sibling rivalry. Raiden and Snake eventually get drawn unwillingly into the argument.

Emma's **Second** Swim

After Emma explains everything Raiden ever wanted to know about computer viruses, swim through the first water area, stopping at every skylight. When you reach the elevator area, the floor is covered with sea lice. Emma won't cross the path. You'll have to consult your peers to figure out what to do here.

Coercing Emma

140.85

COLONEL

Talk to the Colonel a few times. After you cut through the conversations about how to lead Emma around, Campbell half jokingly suggests knocking Emma unconscious in order to drag her through the bugs.

About Emma Emmerich

141.80

SNAKE

The heated debate continues, but this time Snake isn't turning the frequency over to Otacon. After the little girl tries to boss him around a bit, Snake has a few harsh words of his own for Emma.

Emma's Fear of **Bugs**

If you try to drag Emma through the sea lice a few times, the Ninja's Cell Phone buzzes. The Ninja says you can drive away the sea lice with the Coolant. So now you know two ways to get Emma back up to 1F. Use punches and kicks to knock her unconscious, then drag her through the lice onto the elevator. Or, use the Coolant spray to drive off every last bug. The first method doesn't take as long. Whichever way suits you best, don't miss the new **M4 Bullets** in the south corner of the area.

5 9 8 0 1 0 1 0 0

0 0 3 2 0 0 2 0 0 6 9 | 4 2 3 0 1 0 3 0 0 5 5

Shell 2 Core, 1F Air Purification Room

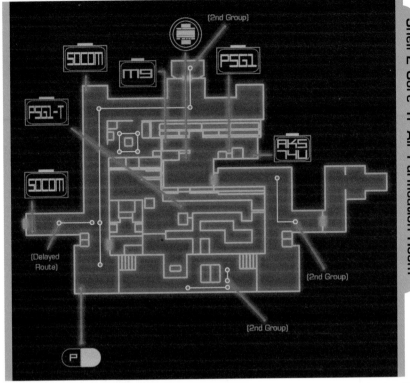

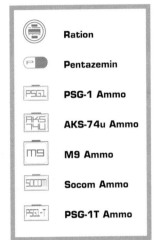

⊟	**Ration**
⊂P⊃	**Pentazemin**
PSG1	**PSG-1 Ammo**
AKS 74U	**AKS-74u Ammo**
M9	**M9 Ammo**
SOCOM	**Socom Ammo**
PSG1-T	**PSG-1T Ammo**

Leave Emma on board the elevator and go take care of the two guards that have taken up patrols on this level. Collect the new items that have appeared here while you're at it. Then lead Emma to the employee break area. New guards will appear as you lead Emma toward the exit, so find good places for her to hide and go take care of business.

Shell 2, 1F Tactics

Crossing the lobby of Shell 2 with Emma is a risky adventure. Raiden must leave Emma in safe locations, then scout ahead to take out enemy guards with extreme prejudice. After you take out guards in this area, shake down their bodies for really good ammo.

DOG TAG: Shell 2 Break Area Guard

Difficulty: Medium

Arriving on 1F, leave Emma on the elevator and scout ahead. There are new **AKS-74u Bullets** to the far east from the elevator. You can easily take the guard patrolling the employee break area when he is facing west. At this location on his route, the guard usually stops and does some stretches. Wait until his cone of vision disappears from the map, then charge at him. After you've arrested the man and confiscated his Dog Tags, execute him with the Socom. It will simplify

matters if you don't have to worry about guards in this area waking up while you are slowly walking Emma around. You should drag the dead body beneath the table in the middle of the break area. New **Socom Bullets** have appeared northwest of the break area.

DOG TAG: Shell 2 South Area Guard

Difficulty: Medium

While Emma is resting on the elevator, go all the way to the south area and stop at the top of the stairs. A guard patrols east to west near the south wall. Wait until he turns and heads off, then move down the stairs and press Raiden's back against the nearest corner. When the guard returns, wait for him to turn and head east again before you run out and

capture him. After you've bagged the tags and killed the guard, drag his body to the west side of the south area. Now you're ready to go back and get Emma off the elevator.

DOG TAG: Shell 2 Malfunctioning Door Guard

Difficulty: Easy

Get Emma off the elevator and lead her into the employee break area. You should notice a guard's cone of vision in the corridor to the south. Leave Emma and quickly run down to the small corridor with the malfunctioning west door. The guard stands and stares transfixed at the door for long periods, allowing ample time to catch him from behind. After you have captured his tags and shot him in the face, collect the **Socom Bullets** that have appeared by the door. Now return to the break area, collect Emma, and lead her south down the corridor to the top of the stairs.

DOG TAG: Shell 2 North Corridor Guard

Difficulty: Hard

Reaching the top of the west stairs in the south area, a new guard will arrive on the elevator! Leave Emma in the small, dark room at the top of the stairs, and run north with your Socom ready. Just below the break area, stop and watch for the guard in First Person View. He stops and turns at the northwest corner. As he is headed back toward the elevator, cut through the break area and catch him from behind. Execute this guard, and then return to the south area. Notice the new box of **Pentazemin** that has appeared in the southwest corner of the area.

DOG TAG: Shell 2 Vent Shafts Guard

Difficulty: Very Easy

Before taking Emma out of the dark room, head down the stairs into the south area and look for the new guard that follows a very short patrol route near the ventilation shafts. Wait on the other side of the blocks until he is facing north, then run around the block and catch him by surprise. Execute this guard, then run back and take Emma out of the small, dark room.

DOG TAG: Shell 2 Exit Guard

Difficulty: Medium

As Raiden and Emma cross the south area and climb the stairs on the east side, let go of her hand and move behind the boxes stacked below the exit corridor. A new guard will emerge from the exit area. After he stares around for what seems like an eternity, he turns north and heads toward the formerly electrified floor. This is when you can easily get the drop on him. You can tranquilize this guard if you wish, because you're about to leave.

KL Connecting Bridge

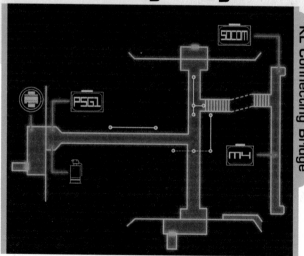

KL Connecting Bridge

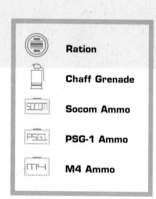

🔘	**Ration**
	Chaff Grenade
SOCOM	**Socom Ammo**
PSG1	**PSG-1 Ammo**
M4	**M4 Ammo**

2 0 0 1 5 9 8 0 1 0 1 0 0 2 1 4 0 0
| 10 | 010 | 101 | 111 | 20 | 020 |

Leave Emma just outside the door while you scout ahead. Stand just outside the doorway and shoot the two Gun Cyphers from a distance before they spot you. Then grab the items around the doorway, including a new **Ration**, **PSG-1 Bullets**, and **Chaff Grenades**.

Cross the connecting bridge to the main bridge, where a soldier will suddenly appear. After you take him out, search the lower bridge for **Socom Bullets** and **M4 Bullets**.

Put out the fire in front of Strut L with the Coolant, and lead Emma across. At the Strut L entrance, Emma gives Raiden the **Lv5 PAN Card**.

KL Connecting Bridge Tactics

The soldier on the bridge can easily spot Raiden if he leads Emma out there carelessly. Scout ahead and clear the entire area of enemies before taking Emma onto the bridge.

DOG TAG: KL Connecting Bridge Guard

Difficulty: Medium

Cross the connecting bridge to the main bridge, and crouch behind the low wall on the north side. Crouch-step to the corner and study the guard's movements behind you. When he faces the stairs on the right, stand and run out from behind the corner. Capture him, and then move to the top of the stairs in front of him. The guard resists arrest, so shoot him in the hand to get the tags. Then execute the guard, because you'll still be in the area for a while collecting items and dousing fires.

Strut L Sewage Treatment Facility

Socom Ammo

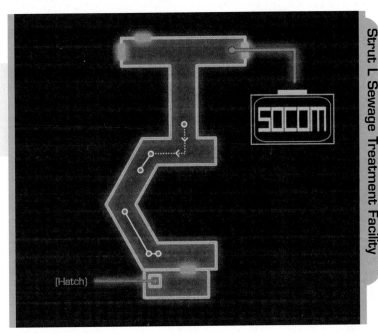

Strut L Sewage Treatment Facility

Leave Emma near the entrance and scout ahead. **Socom Bullets** are at the end of the hall. Two guards are inside the main room; both have Dog Tags. These are some of the most difficult guards in the game to hold up, so best of luck getting those tags! See the following Tactics section.

Once you've got the guards bedded down, take Emma south to the watertight door and move over to the floor hatch.

MISSION 6: THE CHILD GENIUS **135**

Strut L Tactics

Taking out these guards is not a real task. Move into the corridor just slightly and target the guard on the far side with the M9. Once that guard is asleep, the other guard will notice and move over to investigate. That's when you should knock him out, too. But if you want their Dog Tags, get ready for the hardest combined Dog Tag strategy in the game!

DOG TAG: Strut L Guards (Both)

Difficulty: Very Hard

First, equip the M9 and tranquilize the guard on the opposite side. Now quickly run forward and wait near the inside wall, just around the corner from the nearest guard. When he turns to patrol the south, run around the corner and catch him. Once you've got his tags, tranquilize him but don't kill him. Drag his body out into the hallway near the exit where you left Emma. Now return to the dozing guard near the watertight door. Spray the Coolant in his face until he starts to wake up. Quickly run back into the hallway, and wait for him to resume his route. This guard is a bit trickier. Watch his route carefully from the safety of the corridor and learn the timing of his movements. When you know that he is at the northern point of his route and about to turn, run in and capture him near the watertight door. Whew—that strategy takes some guts!

Strut L Oil Fence

Emma and Raiden climb down the long ladder outside the base of Strut L. To get back to Shell 1 from here, the two must cross the Oil Fence using the pontoon bridges that connect Strut L to Strut E. In a few minutes, Snake will arrive to give you some backup, but you must handle it on your own for now. Using the sniper rifle, Raiden must clear the way for Emma.

 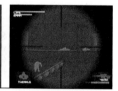

Sniping Tips Revisited

Equip the Thermal Goggles to better see Claymores and sentries. First, shoot the four Claymores nearest Strut L. Then look for sentries on the platform ahead. If they stop, don't zoom in; you want to be able to see if others show up. It's also important to shoot at nerve endings, such as in the shoulder. If you can disable a guard's arm, he can't fire or use his radio. Be sure to double-tap `L2` once in a while to reload the rifle, and check the platform occasionally to see if additional bullets or Pentazemin has appeared adjacent to Raiden's position. Use First Person View to narrow down your initial aim before you raise the sniper rifle's scope to your eye. Finally, laying down on the ground can help steady your aim.

When Emma reaches the first column and starts to cross behind it, you'll need to worry about additional soldiers on the column and Gun Cyphers that might float into view.

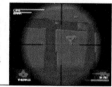

Around this time, Snake will call. You can spot him lying on the upper part of Strut E, willing to help you with the sniping. Just call him on the Codec when you want him to join in, and he will snipe whatever is in your scope. This is especially helpful if you run out of bullets or Pentazemin.

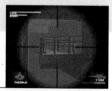

11010

071230154801010031200389

Blast the soldiers and Gun Cyphers around the second column, then look over to the far right side by Strut E. There are two more Claymores on the bridge that you need to shoot, so zoom in close. But don't forget to check on Emma, too.

 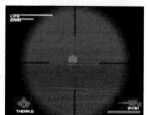

BOSS FIGHT

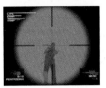

Final Vamp

Gender:	Male
Affiliation:	Dead Cell Knife Specialist
Weapon:	Serrated Hunting Knife

You can't keep a thirsty vampire down. When Emma almost reaches safety, the Romanian knife wizard takes her hostage in a desperate last stand. For Emma's safety, switch over to the PSG-1T. That way, if you hit her by accident, she won't take as much damage. Besides, it's really cool to see 10 or 12 darts sticking out of Vamp's face. You don't need the Thermal Goggles for this, so keep the Pentazemin ready if you have any left—it really comes in handy. Aim for Vamp's head and shoot as rapidly as possible. If you lose your aim on the head, target Vamp's shoulder when he twists Emma to the side. After you have knocked his purple "consciousness bar" down to half, take another Pentazemin even if Raiden still seems steady. When the purple "consciousness bar" under Vamp's life bar runs out, the battle ends.

MISSION 07: DELIVER THE DISK

With Emma seriously wounded, Snake takes the girl and runs ahead to the Shell 1 Computer Room on the B2 level. Raiden crosses the oil bridge on his own and enters the lower level of Strut E. From here, Raiden has 300 seconds to reach the B2 Level of Shell 1.

Strut E Parcel Room B1

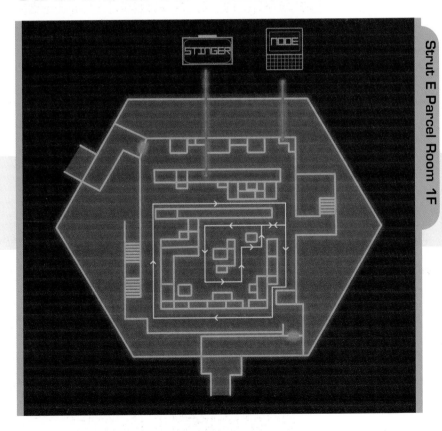

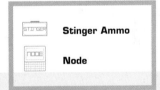

STINGER	Stinger Ammo
NODE	Node

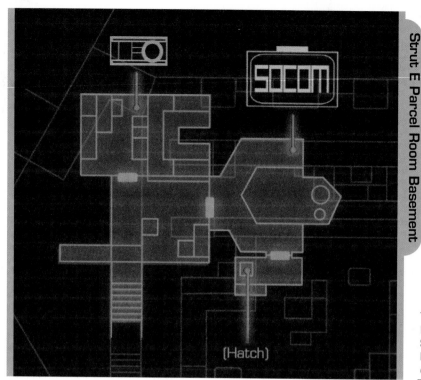

 Digital Camera	
Socom Ammo	

(Hatch)

The clock is ticking, so get a move on! You have 300 seconds to reach the B2 level of Shell 1. **Socom Bullets** are at the top of the B1 platform. Exit through the Lv5 door, and enter the other one in the corridor.

Say Cheese!

The **Digital Camera** is in the small parcel storage room. While it's a little late to start taking pictures, this item will be mighty helpful in your next game. Check the Secrets and Bonuses section of this guide for more details.

Run up to the first floor, but be wary of the new guard left behind to patrol this area. He is listening to music and distracted, but still reacts to the sight of Raiden. Once you've sneaked up and claimed his tags, move to the conveyor close to the DE Connecting Bridge entrance. Crawl under the machine to find a new box of **Stinger Missiles**, and claim any other ammo you didn't get on previous trips through here.

Parcel Room Tactics

The lone soldier in this area is distracted by his music, so it should be quite easy to cap him from a distance. Sneaking up behind him is quite another matter. Once he's tranquilized, you might be able to shake RGB6 shells out of him too!

DOG TAG: Parcel Room Boogie Guard

Difficulty: Medium

The last guard in the game with Dog Tags is deceptively tricky, mostly due to the wide patrol route he follows. The strategy that seems to work the best is to move from the stairs up to the north conveyor, where the missiles are found. Hide behind this conveyor until the music-loving guard crosses the area below. Running around the conveyor, Raiden must capture the guard before he turns and heads south.

EF Connecting Bridge

Destroy two of the three Gun Cyphers in this area from inside the Strut E entrance, then move toward the bridge and look for another Gun Cypher to appear. Once that's been shot down, then cross the bridge. The quickest way across is to side-step down the thin ledge left on either side, and then jump over the last gap.

Shell 1 Core, 1F

Watch out for mines on the south side of the corridor. Move up to the elevator before time runs out. Check your Rations for parasites after you run through the sea lice. Entering the elevator takes Raiden immediately through a series of scenes in the B2 Computer Room. From there, this band of extraordinary men prepares to enter the freight elevator, which descends deep into Arsenal Gear.

MISSION 08: ARSENAL GEAR

The victim of a treacherous double-cross, Raiden finds himself in a torture chamber modeled after the one in Shadow Moses. Ocelot isn't in charge of the torture this time—that honor belongs to Solidus. Once you've survived his tentacle grip, a secret ally breaks Raiden free. Naked and weaponless, Raiden must rely purely on his skills of evasion to get through Arsenal unscathed.

Arsenal Gear: Stomach

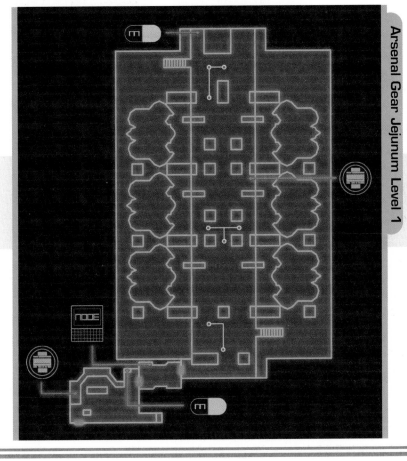

Arsenal Gear Jejunum Level 1

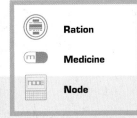

	Ration
m	Medicine
node	Node

4 0 1 3 2 9 5 0 0 1 0 0 2 1 4 8 6 0 1 8 7
4 7 8 7 3 7 0 5 0 1 1

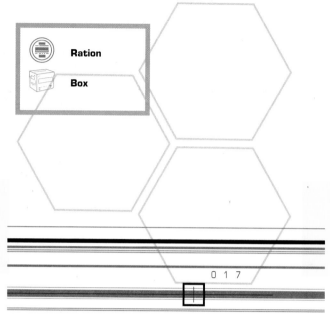

Ration

Box

0 1 7

Afterward, Olga socks Raiden in the stomach for a few points of damage. When Raiden is alone, moving left or right causes him to yank against his restraints. The only point of outside contact is the Colonel, who commands him to stay put. After a few minutes of staring at the walls, Rose calls and Raiden is released. Snake is waiting for Raiden at the end of a long corridor full of guards. Getting through this long and open area alone is the challenge of a lifetime.

Raiden finds himself strapped to a torture table facing Ocelot and Solidus. During the torture event, tap ⃝ as quickly as you can to avoid losing any health.

Once you're released from the manacles, move to the locker near the exit and find the **Medicine** inside. If Raiden runs around naked for an extended period, he will start sneezing. Use the Medicine to cure his cold, so that he does not accidentally give away his position. Outside the torture room door, download the Soliton Radar map from the local network Node.

The 'Bare' Essentials

With one hand occupied covering his privates, Raiden's abilities are seriously compromised. He cannot hang from rails or even fight hand-to-hand very well. He is also unable to perform the chokehold, so don't get caught attempting to do something you're unable to.

Arsenal Gear: Jejunum

Raiden receives a strange message from the Colonel that's somewhat garbled. But a more pressing priority is how to get around the guard patrolling the area outside the Stomach. When the guard turns and moves north, run from Raiden's starting position all the way to the giant cargo container on the right. Flatten Raiden's back against the south edge of the crate and knock on the metal surface to attract the guard's attention. As the guard approaches the crate from the left side, move around the opposite side and continue north. At this point, you have to decide whether you are going to go up the stairs to the right or continue through the lower portion of the Jejunum. We've provided strategy for either choice in the following two sections, starting with the lower level.

Campbell Takes a Holiday

Raiden begins to receive strange transmissions from Colonel Campbell. This strategy guide can't help you anymore, so just throw the book into the garbage and go do your homework. Honestly, though, you've been reading a long time. Black type on white paper does my heart good to see three consecutive all-nighters go to good use. Spaghetti on Wednesday, stop by my freshly cut yard—Snake, watch out! Meryl's not herself! She's under Mantis's mind control!

What's going on here? I need scissors!

Lower Level Subterfuge

If you decide you'd rather ascend the stairs to the right of your current position, skip this section and read the following "Upper Level Hiding" section. If you are moving on through the bottom level, then best of luck to you. Move all the way up to the large container on the right and hide behind it. Sometimes the second guard on the lower level looks north and pauses. At this opportunity, move to the first low container on the right. Crouch and crawl behind it, continuing north. Find a **Ration** just past the next large container on the right.

Move up to the next large container on the right. Start keeping tabs on the position of the guard on the upper level. If the red dot indicating his position is close to the connecting bridge above, do not move for a while. Also, watch the last guard on the lower level. When he is on the west side of the large central container, move to the front of the container and press your back against it. Knock on the container, and the guard will come to investigate. Whichever side he moves to, run around the opposite side of the container and run up the stairs. By the way, there is more **Medicine** in the upper-left corner of the lower level, but you can carry only one.

On the top level, stay behind the large container on the western rail, and peek around the corner at the guard on the opposite side. Study his movement pattern carefully. It will be difficult to get past him, because he patrols directly in front of the exit! Once you have memorized his pattern, move to the bridge and stop. Watch the surveillance camera's cone of vision, and as it moves away from the bridge, run at the camera. Using the blind spot directly beneath the device, move to the south side of the column on which the camera is mounted. Press Raiden's back against it and resume watching the guard near the exit. After he searches near Raiden's location and moves north, run for the exit. Most likely, the guard will notice the movement and come to investigate. However, if you keep running through the exit, there will be no Alert.

Upper Level Hiding

If you've already followed the strategy for investigating the lower level of the Jejunum and you've made it through the exit, skip ahead to the "Arsenal Gear: Ascending Colon" section. However, If you choose to ascend the first set of stairs, there is also a good way to break through on the upper level.

Out in the Open

At all points in the upper level, you must monitor the movements and sight lines of the guards above as well as below. Guards on both levels can see you.

Move from the top of the stairs, across the narrow catwalk, to the west side of the room, where you can reclaim the **Z.O.E. Cardboard Box**. In areas where there is only a camera, simply run under it and navigate close to the column underneath to stay in the device's blind spot. Move up the west side of the room to the middle catwalk bridge and wait for the guard on the other side to move north. Head across the catwalk then, provided that no other sentries are directly below the catwalk bridge, and run as far up behind the guard as you can. Equip the Z.O.E. Box very quickly and remain still as he turns and passes moving south. This doesn't always work; if the Box is too much of an obstruction in the guard's path, he'll likely examine it and discover you. If the Box provides successful cover, then unequip it as soon as the guard passes south of you, and move north from there along the east side of the room. There is a gap in the floor, which you can cross with a torso-axial jump. However, the hole drops down to the location of a **Ration** below.

Across the gap, set down on the other side of the last column, where a camera views the situation overhead. Press Raiden's back against the lower part of the column. Watch the guard near the exit carefully. When he patrols the south area near Raiden's hiding spot and then moves north, run under the camera's blind spot and make a break for the door. The guard will most likely notice something and come to investigate, but you can rush out the exit before he actually confirms sighting Raiden.

Arsenal Gear: Ascending Colon

Run south in the corridor, toward the game camera's position, to find a **Ration**. Then run north. You may notice that a video clip of a girl overtakes the Soliton Radar. If you answer a Codec call, this will disappear. Keep running up and down in the hall and answering the Colonel's weird messages until Rose calls. After the conversation, Solid Snake emerges. Fully decked out in his trademark sneaking suit and bandana, he looks ready to take care of business. He returns all of Raiden's former equipment, plus a little gift from the Ninja, the **High Frequency Blade**.

Get used to the control of the ninja blade now while you have a few minutes. Control the blade using the Right Analog Stick. Press up to execute an uppercut, down to cleave, and left and right to slash from side to side. If you press the stick up or down, Raiden will hold the blade in position until you move the Right Stick again or release it. Press the Right Stick as a button, and Raiden will thrust with the sword. Rotate the Right Stick all the way around, and Raiden will execute a spinning slash. To block, press **L1**. Raiden can even block bullets with the sword. When the sword icon in the right menu is red, the sword will cause damage to an enemy's life bar. Press ⬤ and the sword icon will switch to blue. In this mode, Raiden attacks with the blunt edge of the sword and knocks enemies unconscious. Blunt mode has only one particular use...

DOG TAG: Solid Snake
Difficulty: Extremely Hard

The final Dog Tags of the game are the hardest to come by, because you have to obtain them from the one and only legendary counter-terrorist, Solid Snake! To get Snake's Dog Tags, switch the HF Sword over to the blunt edge. Attack Snake with the sword, then run away. Snake gets angry and will attack with punches and kicks. He will even draw his Socom and fire! Dodge his attacks using Raiden's torso-axial jump. If possible, use the jump to hurt Snake, as well. After Snake has taken a series of blunt strikes, he will be knocked unconscious. Shake down his body to make his tags drop out.

Arsenal Gear: Ileum

Together, Snake and Raiden will have to blast their way through tons of soldiers in the minutes to come. Luckily, Snake has his Infinite Ammo Bandana. So, if you run out of bullets, he'll throw you some. Just stick with the same weapon the whole time and stay close to Snake.

Infinite ammo.

0 0 3 2 0 0 2 0 0 6 9

Keep the Rations equipped to avoid dying during the melee. Use a machinegun, such as the M4 or the AKS-74u. Duck behind cubes and rectangles on either side and in the center. To be able to fire as you move, hold L1. Basically, you should charge down the aisle firing, running from cover point to cover point to avoid enemy fire. Use the step-out technique to nail enemies as they cross.

The Arsenal Tengus with the swords will be able to block bullets. Engage them at close range with punches and kicks, and they shouldn't get back up. Also, if Tengus get shot from two different angles, they can't defend themselves.

Use First Person View to take out snipers perched on the rails above. Watch out for falling bodies; they cause damage. When you reach the end of the row, just keep blasting until the all clear chime sounds. Stay close to Snake so that he will throw you more bullets. If Snake dies, the game ends. Don't let him do all the fighting, or he will take all the damage, as well.

Technical Advice

141.12

OTACON

Hal will be your strategic advisor as Raiden and Snake face off against the Tengu hordes. Through various conversations, he will suggest tips for fighting the Tengus and provide extremely accurate technical data on their weapons and armor. He even has tips for how to use the HF Blade against Tengus, but you will take less damage and kill more enemies using a machinegun.

Arsenal Gear: Sigmoid Colon

Grab the **Ration** and move into the next chamber. Tengu Commandos surround Snake and Raiden, so there's no way out but to fight. Again, equip a machinegun. Stay close to Snake so that he can throw you Rations and hopefully ammo. Try not to hit Snake, and flip out of his line of fire. Luckily, he enters this room with another full bar of health.

Stay at the bottom of the screen as much as possible if Snake will allow, since that provides better visibility. Hold **L1** so that Raiden can fire and keep moving, which is very important in this circular room.

Use kicks and punches to take out Sword Tengus. If the ammo seems to stop coming and Raiden runs out, switch over to a fun weapon like the RGB6. Start blowing up clusters of enemies, but don't let Snake get caught in the blast.

Another good way to break through this chamber of death in style is to use the HF Blade. Press **L1** to block bullets from the front, and get used to fighting with the sword. You practically have to be an expert with the sword by the time you reach the final battle.

Fission Mailed?

A few times during the fight, a facsimile of the Game Over screen will appear. This is just Arsenal's AI messing with Raiden's head some more. We suggest sitting really close to the screen and keeping close tabs on the fight because the battle will continue, even while this frustrating interference is in effect.

Final Battles Ahead!

Try not to consume too many Rations during all the wetworks. After the firefights, you'll face a major skirmish with a deployment of Metal Gear RAYs, followed by an even more intense final showdown!

Arsenal Gear: Rectum

Arsenal Gear: Rectum

Raiden climbs the ladder out of the Sigmoid Colon, arriving at a level that seems ripped straight from one of his VR training missions. As you listen to Solidus's voice, consider using your time to equip the HR Blade and practice your moves. While this is not yet the final boss fight, the HR Blade will be the *only* weapon you can use when that time comes, so you must become proficient with it quickly.

BOSS FIGHT

Metal Gear RAY Army

Contact Otacon frequently at the start of the battle. He provides some of the clues and strategies listed here. Equip the Rations and the Chaff Grenades. Raiden can run while throwing a Chaff. The electronic jamming will make it harder for the RAYs to hit Raiden with missiles, and they will be unable to lock on with their machineguns.

You can avoid machinegun and missile attacks by performing the torso-axial jump at just the right instant. RAYs have different warnings for each type of attack. The machinegun attack comes after a RAY hides its head behind its arm for a moment. When a RAY launches homing missiles, Raiden can hear the sonar targeting lock of their guidance system. Before a RAY fires its rail gun, it must open its faceplate and draw in outside energy. The only attack that really comes with little warning is when a RAY fires missiles from its knees. But you can avoid this attack by using the Chaff Grenades and staying close to RAYs that have jumped into the ring with Raiden.

After you have set off a Chaff Grenade, equip the Stinger Missile Launcher. You'll notice targets outlined at the RAY's knees and head. The way to attack a RAY and cause maximum damage is to fire one missile at the knee, then one at the head. When a RAY is hit in the knee, it buckles over from the impact. The head will lean over the impacted knee and the faceplate will open. So, after you have fired a missile at the knee, raise the Stinger's scope just slightly, and the head should fall into the lock-on area. Missiles that strike a RAY's head while its faceplate is open inflict a tremendous amount of damage.

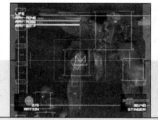 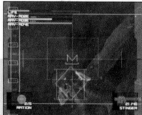

After you've reduced one of the RAYs to half its health, it will jump into the central ring with Raiden. By jumping away at just the right moment, Raiden can avoid damage from the force of this entrance. The RAYs' strategy shifts at this point. While the RAY inside the ring attacks with machinegun, rail gun, and knee-fired missiles, the RAYs outside the ring will target homing missiles at Raiden. By staying in fairly close range of the RAY inside the arena, the RAYs outside the ring won't risk firing missiles. If you continually throw Chaff Grenades to maintain the electronic interference, then the only attack you have to worry about from the RAY in the ring is the rail gun, and possibly an occasional stomp of its feet.

11010

071230154801010031200389

607201208868

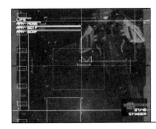

Target the RAY inside the ring with the Stinger, continuing the same strategy of shooting the knee and then the open face. After each successful attack, unequip the Stinger and move. If you are short on Rations, sometimes one will spawn in the center of the arena. Stinger Missiles will appear on the outskirts of the ring when Raiden gets low.

To survive this battle, you must destroy the first five RAYs that appear. These are designated consecutively RAY-RO1E through RAY-RO5E. If you read the name of the last RAY with interpretation, the battle will end when Metal Gear ROSE is destroyed. So if things aren't going well, find and defeat this gear to end the battle more quickly.

MISSION 09: SONS OF LIBERTY

Solidus and Raiden face off on the roof of New York's earliest monument, Federal Hall. Solidus uses the might of his experimental U.S. Army power suit, equipped with missile-launching tentacles. Rayden has only his skill and his HF Blade.

BOSS FIGHT

Solidus

Otacon is still available by Codec to provide Raiden tips on how to beat Solidus. The strategy covered here will supplement Otacon's advice.

The way to survive this battle is to use L1 effectively and plan a series of counterstrikes and escapes at key moments. A **Ration** sits in the upper-front corner of Federal Hall's roof, and that's all you get. Equip your remaining Rations in the left menu, and keep the HF Blade in sharp edge mode (red). Charge at Solidus, holding L1 to block his sword swipes. After Solidus's swords have bounced off Raiden's defense, he will have overextended himself. The most damaging attack Raiden can inflict is to combine a series of up and down, left and right slashes. Don't try anything too fancy, like the spin move. As Raiden continues to slash, he will gradually turn left or right. Press L1 and Raiden will auto-face Solidus while defending himself. Because Solidus is missing his left eye, he is less likely to see and defend against attacks from his left.

There are a few attacks that Raiden cannot defend against. When Solidus streaks across the roof, leaving a trail of fire in his wake, only luck will prevent Raiden from being set ablaze. Being on fire will continually reduce Raiden's health, so keep doing torso-axial rolls to shake out the flames. Use this move to jump over streaks of fire, as well. During the first round of the battle, Solidus often follows up a fire streak with a volley of tentacle missiles. Hold **L1** and charge at Solidus, and the blade should deflect the missiles. This positions Raiden for an excellent counterstrike opportunity. When Solidus leaps onto the wall of the connecting building, run away! The megalomaniac will land with tremendous force, knocking Raiden to the ground. If one of Solidus's tentacles manages to grab Raiden, press △ rapidly and wiggle the Left Analog Stick to get free.

After Raiden has reduced the wretch's life bar by half, Solidus casts off the tentacles. Doing so increases the speed of his fire streak attack. Solidus will streak around the roof, setting the entire area ablaze. Then he will taunt Raiden and streak directly at him, delivering an unbelievable power punch. The key to avoiding this attack is to stay in one place while Solidus is fire-streaking around and prepare for the final charge. Raiden must flip out of the way at just the right moment. If you do this correctly, Raiden should be positioned near Solidus's side or back for an excellent counterstrike opportunity. How do you prevent Solidus from repeatedly streaking all over the place? During the second round, you must focus on engaging Solidus at close range. If Raiden can keep him busy, then he will not have the chance to start a triple fire streak. Defend against Solidus's sword slashes and counterstrike when he has overextended himself.

1024013295001002148 6 0187
0 1 4 7 8 7 3 7 0 5 0 1 1

Mission **Complete**

This Mission Analysis contains the keys to the future. What you do with those keys is up to you. No one can make your decisions for you. Life is too short and too precious to let anyone control you. Take control by using the strategies you've been given and unlock the secrets of the Patriots by turning to the next chapter.

ZHEA FBSL IEZV LK6S
ROXA TZEMZO

300010

97001236

02001255

SECRETS AND BONUSES

Conquering *Metal Gear Solid 2* is only the beginning. There are several dozen secrets in the game, which serve as interesting and amusing nuances that encourage playing through the game multiple times. There are also secret items and hidden modes of play that you can open by completing the game. Following are just a few of the game's many secrets. How many more can you find?

GAME NUANCES

This section lists a lot of the little things you might have missed while playing *Metal Gear Solid 2* the first time through. They are all available to see during your first game if you have a keen eye.

Title Screen Titillation

While you're staring at the title screen and Snake's red mug, you can manipulate the background's position and color by moving the Right Analog Stick. Press L2 and a gunshot will sound.

Codec Craziness

While watching any Codec conversation, move the Right and Left Analog Sticks and the characters' faces will move. Press on the sticks, and the faces will zoom in close. Press the R1 or R2 button while Snake or Raiden is listening to someone, and you can hear their thoughts. Some of the guys' secret attitudes toward the other characters are quite funny!

Camera Surveillance

Equip the Scope, the Camera, or the Digital Camera and watch soldiers from a distance. Press the Action button and something strange but useful happens; if you have collected that soldier's Dog Tags, his name will be displayed. This helps you determine which guards remain to be captured.

Different Olga Cinemas

Depending on which side of the Port Navigational Deck you defeat Olga Gurlukovich during the "Tanker" episode, the cinema afterward changes slightly. If you defeat her on the left side of the area, she is seen hanging over the rail in the cinema. Defeat her on the right side, and she is slumped against an open crate. All of the camera angles are changed accordingly.

Cinema Control

During any of the cinemas depicting real-time events in the game, press the R1 button to zoom in on the scene. Then move the Right Analog Stick to move the camera. This is a great way to examine the fantastic amount of detail in the character modeling and background textures.

Calisthenics

Either character can improve the level of his Grip Gauge by doing chin-ups from a rail. To do this, hang over the rail and press L2 and R2 simultaneously to exercise. Do 100 chin-ups, and the Grip Gauge will increase in level. The gauge can reach Level 3 by doing a certain number of chin-ups.

Perverted Troopers

Leave open one of the lockers with a pinup on Deck-A of the Tanker. If soldiers come into the room on a "clearing" mission, they will stop and gawk at the pretty lady. We don't want to repeat the noises they make...

Tanker Shortcuts

Use First Person Mode at the top of the Engine Room, and you'll notice a wire that extends from one side of the room to the other. Leap over the back rail and shimmy onto the wire. It helps if you have a leveled-up Grip Gauge!

When sneaking into the cargo holds, look for hatches at the back of each room. There is a hatch that Snake can climb into at the back of Hold No.1. Crawl through the vent into Hold No.2, and look for another hatch on the other side of the projectors. Crawl through this vent, and you'll reach Hold No.3 with no problems! Also, look for wires that span the upper levels of the holds...

Photo Evidence

During the "Tanker" episode, use the Camera to take pictures of things like the pinups in the lockers, Olga sleeping, the muscular chest on the outside of the locker, and the Vulcan Raven action figure. You know you have a worthy shot when Snake makes a sound or says something. Play through the "Tanker" chapter without restarting the game, and when you reach Hold No.3, transmit your photos to Otacon. His reactions to these kinds of photos are very amusing.

Seagull Splatter

If you look up in the sky in First Person View and a bird flies overhead, droppings will land right on the camera!

Shave, Snake!

At the beginning of the "Plant" chapter, hop over the rail of the pool and shimmy over to the area that contains the deep sea diving suits. Jump over the rail into the area and collect the **Shaver**. When Raiden meets Snake, he will tell him to use it. Not only is Snake's reaction amusing, but it will change his appearance in later cinemas as well.

Parcel Travel

Hop onto the conveyor on the east side of the Strut E Parcel Room and equip any Cardboard Box. You can ride the conveyor belt around the Big Shell. The box you equip determines where you are transported. The box marked "The Orange" takes you to Strut C, and the *Zone of the Enders* box takes you to the small room below where the Digital Camera is located. This is a good way to get the camera earlier in the game. Try using the other boxes and see where you end up!

Flashback Photos

In one of the flashback cinemas during the "Plant" episode, you will see the photos *you* took during the "Tanker" episode. Also, if you threw any guards overboard or knocked them over the railing, photos of this will be shown as well.

Hidden Books

There are five Books hidden above a locker on the west side of the Shell 1 Core's B2 level. Punch the locker until the door falls off, and the Books will fall from atop the lockers!

Nature Calls

Move around the Strut L Perimeter undetected, and a guard will start to pee off the side of the building. If you look up in First Person View, you can see Raiden is getting sprinkled. If you fire a warning shot upward at him, the guard will stop for a moment. When he decides the coast is clear, he goes right back to business.

Very Easy... Too Easy!

In Very Easy Difficulty, you only have to access the Node once. All areas will appear on the Soliton Radar automatically for the rest of the game.

Steaming Stillman

When Stillman hides in the pantry, knock on the door or try to open the door. He responds each time. If you do this eight times, his reactions become quite amusing.

Fatman Fun

During the Fatman boss fight, watch for him to become stationary. Stop and watch him in First Person View. When Fatman is having fun with the seagulls, if one of them lands on his collar, it will peck at his head. Also, when Fatman is skating, it only takes one shot at his inline skates to knock him down.

Birdie Talk

The parrot in the Shell 1 Core's B2 Computer Room is fun to mess around with. If you fire bullets at it or spray the Coolant at the bird, it will imitate one of the guard's voices. If any of them are nearby, they will be instantly alerted! If two enemy soldiers stop and have a conversation in the upper portion of the room, wait until they are finished. Then go back to the parrot and view it in First Person. It will repeat their conversation, which reveals clues about where to find some hidden dirty books!

Easter Island Statues

There are four Easter Island MOAI statues that decorate various areas in the game. Use First Person View in every area to search for them.

Floating Debris

In the underwater areas of the Shell 2 Core, Filtration Chamber 1, swim to the last skylight at the south end of the west corridor and surface. There's a rubber ducky floating on the water, which represents a little inside humor.

In the corridor leading to the last area of Chamber 1, there is a second Vulcan Raven Action Figure floating near the doorway.

003 200 20 069 | 4 2 3 0 1 0 3 0 0 5 5

More Arsenal Gibberish

If you are killed in Arsenal Gear and use a Continue, when Raiden reenters the area the name will be displayed in gibberish.

Imprinted Dog Tags

At the end of the game, the information that you entered during the first login to the Node will appear on Raiden's Dog Tags, nicely imprinted into the metal.

Radar Weather Girl

When Raiden is waiting for Snake in the Arsenal Gear corridor, a short video featuring a Konami Eyes model will suddenly overtake the Soliton Radar display. Don't answer a Codec call while the video is playing, or it will disappear.

1 0 2 4 0 1 3 2 9 5 0 0 1 0 0 2 1 4 8 6 0 1 8 7

REPLAY VALUES

Following are things you'll notice about *Metal Gear Solid 2* in a replay game.

Clear Code

Jot down the code at the end of any episode. Then go to the *Metal Gear Solid 2* website at **www.konamijpn.com** and input the code. Your code contains information about your ranking, which will be displayed for you.

To receive a better clear code, replay the entire game and move with better stealth. Complete the harder difficulty levels, finish the entire game quickly, don't kill anyone you don't have to, don't use a Continue, and don't save your game. Your ranking is a summary of everything you see on the Result screen after the credits.

Episode Choice

After completing the game, the title of your save will be red. Load this game in order to play with the new items you received. Whether you load the clear game or start a brand new game, you can now play a full game over again, or you can play either the "Tanker" or the "Plant" chapter alone. Completing either of these shorter versions of the game allows you to receive a ranking and the Digital Camera, but not any other bonus items.

Different Title Screen

Clear the game once, and the title screen will feature a blue image of Raiden. Clear the game again, and it goes back to Snake's red face. Metal Gear RAY can be seen in the background of the next screen.

Standing at Attention

During your second game, all the Marines in the last Hold of the Tanker will be missing their trousers.

Skip the Dialogue

Certain scenes that you couldn't skip in your first game can be skipped in replay games. Press START or to skip a scene.

BONUS ITEMS

When you play through the game a certain way and then start a new game, your character will have new items in the inventory.

Digital Camera

Complete the game at any difficulty level, and you'll be able to replay the "Tanker-Plant" episode with the Digital Camera already in your inventory. To get the Digital Camera in the individual episodes, you'll have to clear each one individually.

Infinite Ammo Bandana

Collect every soldier's Dog Tags in the "Tanker-Plant" game, and start a new game from this save. Snake's inventory includes the Infinite Ammo Bandana. He never has to reload and never runs out of bullets.

Wigs

Collect every soldier's Dog Tags in the "Tanker-Plant" game, and start a new game from this save. Raiden has a Wig in his inventory. Wearing this, he never runs out of ammo and he never has to reload.

There are two other Wigs that Raiden can get, each of which gives him immunity in some other way. See if you can infiltrate deep enough to uncover them...

DOG TAG CHECKLIST

Tanker Chapter: U.S.S. Discovery

DIFFICULTY SETTING: VERY EASY

✓	DOG TAG	LOCATION
	000	Navigational Deck, Wing
✓	001	Aft Deck
✓	002	
✓	003	
	004	Navigational Deck, Wing
✓	005	Deck-A, Crew's Quarters
✓	006	Deck-B, Crew's Quarters
	007	Deck-A, Crew's Lounge
	008	
	009	
	010	Deck-D, Crew's Quarters
	011	
	012	Deck2, Port
	013	
	014	
	015	Engine Room
	016	
	017	
	018	
	019	

DIFFICULTY SETTING: EASY

✓	DOG TAG	LOCATION
	000	Navigational Deck, Wing
	001	Aft Deck
	002	
	003	
	004	Navigational Deck, Wing
	005	Deck-A, Crew's Quarters
	006	Deck-B, Crew's Quarters
	007	Deck-A, Crew's Lounge
	008	
	009	
	010	Deck-D, Crew's Quarters
	011	
	012	Deck2, Port
	013	
	014	
	015	Engine Room
	016	
	017	
	018	
	019	
	020	

DIFFICULTY SETTING: NORMAL

✓	DOG TAG	LOCATION
	000	Navigational Deck, Wing
	001	Aft Deck
	002	
	003	
	004	Navigational Deck, Wing
	005	Deck-C, Crew's Quarters
	006	Deck-A, Crew's Quarters
	007	Deck-B, Crew's Quarters
	008	
	009	Deck-A, Crew's Lounge
	010	
	011	
	012	Deck-D, Crew's Quarters
	013	
	014	
	015	Deck2, Port
	016	
	017	
	018	Engine Room
	019	
	020	
	021	
	022	
	023	
	024	

DIFFICULTY SETTING: HARD

✓	DOG TAG	LOCATION
	000	Navigational Deck, Wing
	001	Aft Deck
	002	
	003	
	004	Navigational Deck, Wing
	005	Deck-C, Crew's Quarters
	006	Deck-A, Crew's Quarters
	007	Deck-B, Crew's Quarters
	008	
	009	Deck-A, Crew's Lounge
	010	
	011	
	012	Deck-D, Crew's Quarters
	013	
	014	
	015	
	016	Deck2, Port
	017	
	018	
	019	Engine Room
	020	
	021	
	022	
	023	
	024	
	025	

✓	DOG TAG	LOCATION
	000	Navigational Deck, Wing
	001	Aft Deck
	002	
	003	
	004	Navigational Deck, Wing
	005	Deck-C, Crew's Quarters
	006	Deck-A, Crew's Quarters
	007	Deck-B, Crew's Quarters
	008	
	009	Deck-A, Crew's Lounge
	010	
	011	
	012	Deck-D, Crew's Quarters
	013	
	014	
	015	

✓	DOG TAG	LOCATION
	016	Deck2, Port
	017	
	018	
	019	Engine Room
	020	
	021	
	022	
	023	
	024	
	025	

Plant Chapter: Big Shell Facility

DIFFICULTY SETTING: VERY EASY

✓	DOG TAG	LOCATION
	000	Arsenal Gear – Ascending Colon
	001	Strut A Deep Sea Dock
	002	
	003	Strut A Roof
	004	Strut A Pump Room
	005	
	006	AB Connecting Bridge
	007	
	008	Strut B Transformer Room
	009	
	010	BC Connecting Bridge
	011	Strut C Dining Hall
	012	
	013	CD Connecting Bridge
	014	
	015	Strut D Sediment Pool
	016	
	017	DE Connecting Bridge
	018	
	019	Strut E Parcel Room
	020	
	021	Strut E Heliport
	022	
	023	Strut F warehouse
	024	
	025	FA Connecting Bridge
	026	Shell 1 Core, 1F
	027	
	028	
	029	Shell 1 Core, B1
	030	
	031	
	032	Shell 1 Core, B2 Computer Room
	033	
	034	
	035	
	036	KL Connecting Bridge
	037	Strut L Sewage Treatment Facility
	038	
	039	Shell 2 Core, 1F Air Purification Room
	040	
	041	
	042	Strut E Heliport

DIFFICULTY SETTING: EASY

✓	DOG TAG	LOCATION
	000	Arsenal Gear – Ascending Colon
	001	Strut A Deep Sea Dock
	002	
	003	Strut A Roof
	004	Strut A Pump Room
	005	
	006	AB Connecting Bridge
	007	
	008	Strut B Transformer Room
	009	
	010	BC Connecting Bridge
	011	Strut C Dining Hall
	012	
	013	CD Connecting Bridge
	014	
	015	Strut D Sediment Pool
	016	
	017	
	018	DE Connecting Bridge
	019	
	020	Strut E Parcel Room
	021	
	022	Strut E Heliport
	023	
	024	Strut F Warehouse
	025	
	026	
	027	FA Connecting Bridge
	028	Shell 1 Core, 1F
	029	
	030	
	031	Shell 1 Core, B1
	032	
	033	
	034	Shell 1 Core, B2 Computer Room
	035	
	036	
	037	
	038	KL Connecting Bridge
	039	Strut L Sewage Treatment Facility
	040	
	041	Shell 2 Core, 1F Air Purification Room
	042	
	043	
	044	Strut E Heliport

DIFFICULTY SETTING: NORMAL

✓	DOG TAG	LOCATION
	000	Arsenal Gear – Ascending Colon
	001	Strut A Roof
	002	Strut A Pump Room
	003	
	004	AB Connecting Bridge
	005	
	006	Strut B Transformer Room
	007	
	008	BC Connecting Bridge
	009	Strut C Dining Hall
	010	
	011	CD Connecting Bridge
	012	
	013	Strut D Sediment Pool
	014	
	015	
	016	DE Connecting Bridge
	017	
	018	Strut E Parcel Room
	019	
	020	
	021	Strut E Heliport
	022	
	023	
	024	Strut F Warehouse
	025	
	026	
	027	FA Connecting Bridge
	028	Shell 1 Core, 1F
	029	
	030	
	031	
	032	Shell 1 Core, B1
	033	
	034	
	035	Shell 1 Core, B2 Computer Room
	036	
	037	
	038	
	039	KL Connecting Bridge
	040	Strut L Sewage Treatment Facility
	041	
	042	Shell 2 Core, 1F Air Purification Room
	043	
	044	
	045	
	046	
	047	
	048	Strut E Heliport

DIFFICULTY SETTING: HARD

✓	DOG TAG	LOCATION
	000	Arsenal Gear – Ascending Colon
	001	Strut A Roof
	002	Strut A Pump Room
	003	
	004	AB Connecting Bridge
	005	
	006	Strut B Transformer Room
	007	
	008	BC Connecting Bridge
	009	Strut C Dining Hall
	010	
	011	CD Connecting Bridge
	012	
	013	Strut D Sediment Pool
	014	
	015	
	016	
	017	DE Connecting Bridge
	018	
	019	Strut E Parcel Room
	020	
	021	
	022	
	023	Strut E Heliport
	024	
	025	
	026	Strut F Warehouse
	027	
	028	
	029	
	030	FA Connecting Bridge
	031	Shell 1 Core, 1F
	032	
	033	
	034	
	035	Shell 1 Core, B1
	036	
	037	
	038	Shell 1 Core, B2 Computer Room
	039	
	040	
	041	
	042	KL Connecting Bridge
	043	Strut L Sewage Treatment Facility
	044	
	045	Shell 2 Core, 1F Air Purification Room
	046	
	047	
	048	
	049	
	050	
	051	Strut E Heliport

✓	DOG TAG	LOCATION
	000	Arsenal Gear – Ascending Colon
	001	Strut A Roof
	002	Strut A Pump Room
	003	
	004	AB Connecting Bridge
	005	
	006	Strut B Transformer Room
	007	
	008	BC Connecting Bridge
	009	Strut C Dining Hall
	010	
	011	CD Connecting Bridge
	012	
	013	Strut D Sediment Pool
	014	
	015	
	016	
	017	DE Connecting Bridge
	018	
	019	Strut E Parcel Room
	020	
	021	
	022	
	023	
	024	Strut E Heliport
	025	
	026	
	027	Strut F Warehouse
	028	
	029	
	030	
	031	
	032	FA Connecting Bridge
	033	Shell 1 Core, 1F
	034	
	035	
	036	
	037	Shell 1 Core, B1
	038	
	039	
	040	Shell 1 Core, B2 Computer Room
	041	
	042	
	043	
	044	KL Connecting Bridge
	045	Strut L Sewage Treatment Facility
	046	
	047	Shell 2 Core, 1F Air Purification Room
	048	
	049	
	050	
	051	
	052	
	053	Strut E Heliport

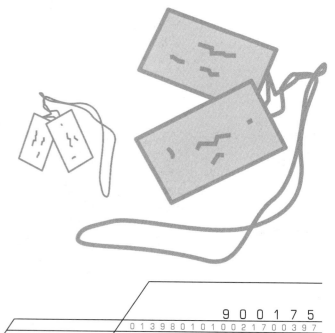

900175

0 1 3 9 8 0 1 0 1 0 0 2 1 7 0 0 3 9 7

1 1 3 7 0   0 2 0 0 6

PHOTO ALBUM

Just because your insertions into the Tanker and the Big Shell aren't officially classified as sightseeing missions, that doesn't mean you can't have a little fun! Once you play through the game, you start subsequent replay games with the Digital Camera in your inventory, which allows you to save snapshots to your memory card. *Metal Gear Solid 2* is filled with interesting and, shall we say, "picturesque" scenes and objects. Here are just a few pictures we snapped during our journeys. Shoot a few of your own and create an album to chronicle your favorite Metal Gear moments!

Jungle babe.

Lady in red.

Olga alerted.

Shells flying in the pantry.

Vulcan Raven with his new toy.

Mooch and friend.

"Hmmm...
I think I forgot something
this morning."

A few good men.

The General.

Sleepin' on the job.

Is that your only tattoo?

And, smile...

!

!!

!!!

Looks harmless... For now.

Dog tags, please.

Disgusting!

Your luck is about to run out.

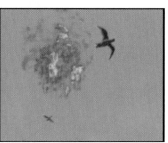
Oh $#!*.

Fatman with pigeons.

Girlie magazine.

Surfin' the net.

Can't get enough.

Policenauts poster.

He looks familiar.

Z.O.E poster.

"Top of locker, top of locker, <squawk>."

Mooch... Again?

Good morning, angels!

Make your own caption.

Revolver Ocelot.

TACTICAL ESPIONAGE ACTION

METAL GEAR SOLID 2
SONS OF LIBERTY

BY DAN BIRLEW

©2002 Pearson Education

BradyGAMES® is a registered trademark of Pearson Education, Inc.

All rights reserved, including the right of reproduction in whole or in part in any form.

BradyGAMES Publishing

An Imprint of Pearson Education
201 West 103rd Street
Indianapolis, Indiana 46290

METAL GEAR ®, METAL GEAR SOLID ® and SONS OF LIBERTY TM are either registered trademarks or trademarks of KONAMI COMPUTER ENTERTAINMENT JAPAN, INC. ©1987 2001 KONAMI COMPUTER ENTERTAINMENT JAPAN. " Ⓩ " and "**KONAMI**®" are registered trademark of KONAMI CORPORATION. All Rights Reserved.

Please be advised that the ESRB rating icons, "E", "RP", "EC", "T", "M", and "AO" are copyrighted works and certification marks owned by the Interactive Digital Software Association and the Entertainment Software Rating Board and may only be used with their permission and authority. Under no circumstances may the rating icons be self-applied to any product that has not been rated by the ESRB. For information regarding whether a product has been rated by the ESRB, please call the ESRB at (212) 759-0700 or 1-800-771-3772. Please note that ESRB ratings only apply to the content of the game itself and do NOT apply to the content of the books.

ISBN: 0-7440-0109-9

Library of Congress Catalog No.: 2001094882

Printing Code: The rightmost double-digit number is the year of the book's printing; the rightmost single-digit number is the number of the book's printing. For example, 01-1 shows that the first printing of the book occurred in 2001.

04 03 02 01   4 3 2 1

Manufactured in the United States of America.

Limits of Liability and Disclaimer of Warranty: THE AUTHOR AND PUBLISHER MAKE NO WARRANTY OF ANY KIND, EXPRESSED OR IMPLIED, WITH REGARD TO THESE PROGRAMS OR THE DOCUMENTATION CONTAINED IN THIS BOOK. THE AUTHOR AND PUBLISHER SPECIFICALLY DISCLAIM ANY WARRANTIES OF MERCHANTABILITY OR FITNESS FOR A PARTICULAR PURPOSE. THE AUTHOR AND PUBLISHER SHALL NOT BE LIABLE IN ANY EVENT FOR INCIDENTAL OR CONSEQUENTIAL DAMAGES IN CONNECTION WITH, OR ARISING OUT OF, THE FURNISHING, PERFORMANCE, OR USE OF THESE PROGRAMS.

BradyGAMES Staff

PUBLISHER
DAVID WAYBRIGHT

EDITOR-IN-CHIEF
H. LEIGH DAVIS

MARKETING MANAGER
JANET ESHENOUR

CREATIVE DIRECTOR
ROBIN LASEK

ASSISTANT LICENSING MANAGER
MIKE DEGLER

ASSISTANT MARKETING MANAGER
SUSIE NIEMAN

Credits

TITLE MANAGER
TIM FITZPATRICK

SCREENSHOT EDITOR
MICHAEL OWEN

LEAD BOOK DESIGNER
CAROL STAMILE

BOOK DESIGNERS
DOUG WILKINS
CHARIS SANTILLIE
DENIS KOSORUKOV
CHRIS LUCKENBILL

PRODUCTION DESIGNERS
TRACY WEHMEYER
CHRIS BERRY

MAPS BY
IDEA + DESIGN WORKS, LLC
WWW.IDEAANDDESIGNWORKS.COM

Acknowledgments

BradyGAMES would like to thank the entire Konami team. Many thanks to Hideo Kojima and the KCEJ Team for producing a Metal Gear title that upholds the tradition of redefining the state of the art. Many thanks to Ken Ogasawara, Tim Vogt and JoJo The Wonder Dog for their gracious assistance and expert game knowledge—this guide would not have been possible without you.

About the Author

Dan Birlew was born in St. Louis, Missouri, and lives in Las Vegas. Dan is the author of fifteen official strategy guides, all published by BradyGAMES, including the Zone of the Enders and Silent Hill 2 official strategy guides. The author would like to acknowledge the contributions of many folks to this guide. Thanks to Ken Ogasawara at Konami for his guidance and support on this text. Special thanks to my wife Laura for working so hard to get the best screenshots possible. And special thanks to my family for checking up on us and showing us how much we are loved.